What does it mean to be a water that bears much fru admire him as I admire fe and friend, I have benefit__ _._..y ui ough tne years from his wise and thoughtful perspective on spiritual formation. If gospel transformation is your goal, you will not be disappointed with this book. The truths presented in *Calling to Christ* will free you, by the Spirit, to "joyfully rest in Christ and live out the special calling" God has just for you.

- Duane David Otto
Pastor, farmer, and Founding President of Ithaka Fellowship – The Agrarian Center for Creation, Culture & Conscience

Bob Smart, fellow-pastor and friend, has that rare blend of being firmly-grounded biblically, theologically, and practically. Even beyond that, his life and writing are both marked with a depth of Christ-connectedness that bleeds through paragraph after paragraph in this book. For anyone wanting clarification about Christian calling and its implications for a life of on-going discipleship, look no further. "Calling to Christ" is the book to read. Bob, like Ezra before him, has set his heart to study the Scriptures, practice them, and teach them wherever and however God gives opportunity. All of that shines through in this book. Read it.

- Dr. J.K. Jones
Pastor of Spiritual Formation, Eastview Christian Church, Normal, IL and Director of the MA in Spiritual Formation, Lincoln Christian University, Graduate Studies, Lincoln, IL.

Robert Smart has been my pastor for more than 21 years. During that time he has faithfully preached the gospel in season and out of season. I have been proud to serve under him at Christ Church as a ruling elder. Dr. Smart has taught the material found in *Calling to Christ* at our church, blessing many, for several years now. I'm passionate about helping people find their callings and am pleased to strongly commend this new book to you.

-Bill Pence
IT Manager at a Fortune 50 organization, Ruling Elder at Christ Church at blogger at Coram Deo the Blog.com

T.S. Elliot asked the question, "Can a lifetime represent a single motive?" For the Christian the answer is yes. God calls for all of me to embrace all of Christ in a life that glorifies and enjoys Him. This is our calling as believers. We have taken our entire church through Dr. Smart's Calling material so that they might understand God's call on their life as much wider than just a vocation. The Calling Study is a fundamental assessment of how Christ's call to the Christian affects all aspects of life. We have seen many people experience Gospel freedom as they realize their primary calling is to a person, before it is to an action or role.

-*Rusty Milton*
Senior pastor Grace Presbyterian Church, Christchurch, New Zealand

Calling to Christ

WHERE'S MY PLACE?

Robert Davis Smart

WESTBOW
PRESS®
A DIVISION OF THOMAS NELSON
& ZONDERVAN

Copyright © 2017 Robert Davis Smart.

All rights reserved. No part of this book may be used or reproduced by any means, graphic, electronic, or mechanical, including photocopying, recording, taping or by any information storage retrieval system without the written permission of the author except in the case of brief quotations embodied in critical articles and reviews.

Unless otherwise indicated, all scripture quotations are from The Holy Bible, English Standard Version (ESV). Copyright 2001 by Crossway Bibles, a division of Good News Publishers. Used by permission. All rights reserved.

WestBow Press books may be ordered through booksellers or by contacting:

WestBow Press
A Division of Thomas Nelson & Zondervan
1663 Liberty Drive
Bloomington, IN 47403
www.westbowpress.com
1 (866) 928-1240

Because of the dynamic nature of the Internet, any web addresses or links contained in this book may have changed since publication and may no longer be valid. The views expressed in this work are solely those of the author and do not necessarily reflect the views of the publisher, and the publisher hereby disclaims any responsibility for them.

Any people depicted in stock imagery provided by Thinkstock are models, and such images are being used for illustrative purposes only.
Certain stock imagery © Thinkstock.

Krista Kuniyoshi, Graphic Designer of "Four Seasons of Spiritual Formation chart" on p. xiii

ISBN: 978-1-5127-8041-3 (sc)
ISBN: 978-1-5127-8039-0 (hc)
ISBN: 978-1-5127-8040-6 (e)

Library of Congress Control Number: 2017904404

Print information available on the last page.

WestBow Press rev. date: 3/22/2017

Contents

Acknowledgments vii
Foreword ix
Introduction: Calling to Christ: The Second of Four Seasons of
    Gospel Transformation xi

Chapter 1   Understanding Our Calling to Christ 1
Chapter 2   The Scriptural and Theological Basis of Calling 15
Chapter 3   Eight Hindrances to Joy in One's Calling 31
Chapter 4   Sensing God's Call on your Life 52
Chapter 5   Living out Your Calling to Christ 68
Chapter 6   Sharing Your Calling to Christ 79

Conclusion: What's the Next Season of Spiritual Formation? 85
Bibliography 87
Appendix: Practicing the Spiritual Discipline of Solitude 93

Acknowledgments

My deep thanks to Christ Church staff and members, *Cru*, *InterVarsity*, and *Navigator* campus staff, and those involved in the last twenty years of spiritual formation classes locally for sharing your precious sense of calling to Christ from the heart. I am also grateful to *Campus Outreach* staff and leaders in Alabama, Louisiana, Illinois, and Texas for using this material. I am indebted to Rev. Rusty Milton of Grace Presbyterian in New Zealand for using this material in local ministry settings, and offering good feedback.

I would also like to acknowledge my appreciation for elders Art Moser and Bob Force for helping me improve this material over the years. Finally, this and many projects could not be possible without the constant encouragement from Gary and Farole Haluska.

Foreword

I can't think of anyone I would rather read than Dr. Bob Smart on the vital topic of discovering one's calling in Christ and flourishing in that calling.

I have known Bob for many years. And I have never known anyone quite like him. Over many decades of walking with the Lord, Bob has become a radiant, calm, and wise man. We have talked together on the phone and in person, prayed together, counseled each other, and encouraged each other.

I trust him. You should too. Bob lives out what he speaks of in these pages. I've seen it. He has faithfully labored in pastoral ministry in central Illinois for many years. Others leaders of his level of gifting often pursue the spotlight and seek out a "platform." Not Bob. He has quietly loved the men and women and children in Normal, Illinois. For this, I esteem him highly. I love him, far beyond other men I know. And one day God is going to put his arm around Bob and introduce him to the world. That will be a sight to behold.

So let Bob coach you in the pages that follow. Life in this fallen world can be so bewildering. We hardly even understand ourselves, let alone others. Who *am* I? How has God wired me? Do I matter? Am I secure? What should I do with my life? If questions like these come to you as you lie in bed at night, this book is for you. Bob will lead you into the still waters and green pastures of settling your identity and calling in the endless grace of the Friend of Sinners, Jesus Christ.

—Dane Ortlund, executive vice president, Crossway

Introduction
Calling to Christ: The Second of Four Seasons of Gospel Transformation

I'll never forget how my dear friend Zack Eswine counseled me when I was a candidate to become the senior pastor for another church. I was afraid—afraid of leaving my present call to the church I had served for so many years, fearful that the new church might not hire me. I was afraid that a move to another place might not be best for my family. I was probably looking for an escape from the place God had put me because of difficult circumstances. Zack's simple statement of truth was very comforting, and it has stayed with me ever since. He said, "Bob, your calling is not at stake."

This book seeks to recover the comforting doctrine of Christian calling in a way that frees Christians from an endless search for the greener grass of another place, and the occasional effort to escape the suffering that awaits us in our present location and vocation. A strong sense of knowing the place and work God has for us is vital in our twenties and thirties. A content and confident Christian, who senses his or her calling to Christ by midlife, brings to others at home and community a message that God is good. It is a season of spiritual formation that sets us up for taking better aim for Christ in our middle years.

In my first book in this series of four on the Christian's spiritual formation, *Embracing Your Identity in Christ: Renouncing Lies and Foolish Strategies*, I wrote:

> Our identity, besides being one of the most precious things to prevent from theft, crisis, or loss, is extremely important to God. The Father has given His each of His children a personal identity in Christ that will shape them on their journey to heaven. If, in the process of identity formation, we ignore what God says concerning our identity, then we may expect confusion in the other three seasons of spiritual formation from adolescence to old age (see chart below for Identity in Christ, Calling to Christ, Intentionality for Christ, and Legacy from Christ).[1]

---

[1] Robert Davis Smart, *Identity in Christ: Renouncing Lies and Foolish Strategies* (Bloomington, IN: Westbow Press, 2017), p. 2.

4 SEASONS OF SPIRITUAL FORMATION

IDENTITY *in* CHRIST
Who am I?

- Names
- Family
- God's Image
- Glorious Ruins
- Renounce Lie
- Justified
- Adopted
- Sanctified

CALLING *to* CHRIST
Where's my place?

- God's Summons
- Central/Peripheral
- Kairotic Events
- 3 Longings
- Micah 6:8
- Prophet/Priest/King
- Apostolic Band
- Agora (Streets)

INTENTIONALITY *for* CHRIST
What's my best aim?

- Gifted & Experienced
- Regrets
- Busyness
- Fear
- Resignation
- Faith/Hope/Love
- Mid-Life Bucket Lists
- Greatest Contribution

LEGACY *from* CHRIST
What's my message?

- My Treasury
- Succession
- Influence
- Will for Others
- The Jordan River
- Benediction
- Deliver Mail
- Letting Go

Just after birth or adoption, a child is given her first sense of identity from her parent(s). Identity formation, however, is a much longer process. When Jesus Christ was approximately thirty years old, the Father spoke of His identity at His baptism just before Jesus entered fully into His primary calling. In the same way, a clear sense of our identity in Christ ought to precede our calling formation to Christ. It is during this foundational season of identity formation that Satan challenges each of us, as he did our Lord. The devil's first attacks were aimed at Jesus's identity when two times he cast doubt about who He was: "*If* you are the Son of God ..." (Luke 4:3, 9)[2].

The evil trinity—the world, the flesh, and the devil—is seeking to kill and destroy us during each of the four seasons of spiritual formation. In the spring, evil confuses our identity; in the summer, our calling; in the autumn, our intentionality; and in the winter, our legacy. The world escorts us to the pit; the flesh entices us to fall in; and the devil pushes us over the edge. "The pit," as it were, represents other voices besides God's telling us what we should do. It is not your place in this season of calling to Christ. It is a place of confusion, greed, and autonomous attempts to make our idealistic dreams of being exceptional come true. It turns darker as unmet longings and failure may lead us down the paths of resignation, romanticism, or self-righteous bitterness. Every Christian is called by the gospel to Christ, which the Father makes effectual at salvation (John 6:44).

This season of spiritual formation for the Christian, Calling to Christ, is the second of four seasons of gospel transformation designed to shape us into the glorious likeness of Jesus Christ. It assumes we have a reasonable grip on our identity in Christ. It also prepares us for the last two seasons of spiritual formation; namely, intentionality and legacy.

This book is designed for group study. A leader or individual will

---

[2] Scripture quotations are from the ESV ® Bible (The Holy Bible, English Standard Version) (Crossway, 2001). Used by permission. All rights reserved.

begin with prayer and then ask the discussion questions provided at the end of each chapter in order to help each person discover and write out a sense of his or her calling to Christ. The goal is that, by the end of the book, each person can use the template provided in the last chapter to write out what he or she senses God's call is to live to the utmost for Christ's glory in all of life. We will purposefully address common pitfalls known to threaten our joy in this second season of spiritual formation with truth and grace, while delighting in the eternal pleasures that await those who "so run" that they may win the prize (1 Corinthians 9:24).

In order to improve upon our effort, chapter 1 explains what it means for a Christian to sense his or her calling to Christ. Chapter 2 addresses the theological foundations for understanding our calling to Christ. Chapter 3 confronts the major hindrances that keep us from clarifying and enjoying our calling to Christ. By confronting such hindrances as romanticism, "vocational shoulds," and resignation, we seek to better hear God's call for us more clearly. In chapter 4, we'll ask God to ask us the three questions of Micah 6:8 and to help us seek to make the most of the kairotic and providential events in our lives. Finally, in chapter 5, we will consider joining others who are in this same place so that our stories may better reflect the gospel.

In all this, we are seeking God's grace—the power of his spirit, the agency of his Word, the mystery of his providence, and the caring concern of his people—to transform each of us more permanently, uniquely, and heartily to answer God's call on our lives.

Wisdom teaches us to begin asking God to give us our identity and our calling before asking the next two major questions of the Christian life: How do I steward all my gifts, resources, and efforts well in the light of eternity (intentionality)? And what inheritance, testament, and benediction do I leave behind as I prepare to cross the river of death and into heaven's gates (legacy)?

When I became a Christian in my early twenties, I was so excited about where God would place me in order to glorify His Name in my calling. Since everything on earth is His, and He has a purpose for everyone, I began to seek Him in prayer for a strong sense of calling. The spiritual formation season for discovering God's call on our life is best discovered in our twenties and thirties.

I finished my college degree and began to realize deep longings for particular callings. One was to marry a godly woman open to my sense of call to the gospel ministry. Although neither had taken place, I had a sense of knowing. So I prayed while working as a branch manager in a bank and participating in a life-on-life missional discipleship movement. At twenty-four I married Karen, at twenty-five we began having children, and by twenty-seven I was in full-time vocational Christian ministry on the college campuses of Purdue University and Ball State University.

This sense of calling became clearer. One day in solitude, engaged in word and prayer, I came across a verse in Proverbs. It is the truism that named how the Holy Spirit uses longings to help us embrace our sense of calling. "A longing realized is sweet to the soul" (Proverbs 13:19). All I knew was that my soul knew the sweetness of a longing to serve God as an expository preacher of scripture, as a pastor of a local church, and to attend Covenant Theological Seminary in Saint Louis, Missouri, for equipping purposes.

Since I was already married with three children, Karen's willingness to embrace her particular calling in relation to mine was essential. After two days of seeking God, Karen also had the same sense of calling in alignment with mine to take the next step of faith. The church we were attending at Ball State University affirmed and recommended me as a candidate for the pastorate too. We had an amazing experience in seminary years of making friends with other students, serving as an intern pastor of a church in Saint Louis, and saturating ourselves with systematic, biblical, and practical theology.

This season of spiritual formation, then, began at twenty-one and lasted until I was about thirty-five—about fifteen years.

Embracing your true sense of calling to Christ carries much more weight than you may give it at the time. The better we become solidified about who God says we are in Christ and about where He is calling us, the more the season of intentionality in our forties and fifties will be fruitful and the season of legacy will be rich in our latter years. It is foundational as an adult, formational during our twenties and thirties, and progressively solidifying for all Christians to become intentional for Christ in the third season of spiritual formation. Finally, we enter the fourth season of spiritual formation, which lasts until we come to cross the river of death with a legacy from Christ. So let's begin with asking what a Christian's calling to Christ really is.

Chapter 1
Understanding Our Calling to Christ

Calling's Question: Where's My Place?

Christians want to discover a sense of calling from God because they no longer live for themselves; rather, they live for, who for their sake died and was raised (2 Corinthians 5:15) Christians have been redeemed, so life is worth living. All of life is meaningful, and even the most ordinary acts of kindness are shot through with eternal consequences (Luke 16:10) Christians want to redeem the time and make the most of our days (Ephesians 5:16) Whatever we do, we do it wholeheartedly as to the Lord—for glory and for our joy (1 Corinthians 10:31; Colossians 3:23–24) This is because our performance for God flows out of our position in Christ. We are accepted as pardoned sinners, righteous children, and saints in Christ (our identities); therefore, we obey (our callings).

Religion, unlike the gospel, reverses this order. Rather than entering into our callings out of a grateful response to Christ's salvation, many are mistakenly trying to perform well enough in their callings to get God to favor and accept them. This is antithetical to the gospel way. We get it all on the front end! Once we receive the free offer of the gospel by faith, all is ours. Therefore, our callings are free from guilty motivations and dreadful fears about whether God loves us or not.

If you are a new creature in Christ and have a solid sense of your identity, the first essential question is settled—namely, who am I in Christ? Now that everything matters and we have been saved from living for ourselves as selfish, autonomous, and arrogant sinners, we sincerely want to ask a very important question in prayer to God through Christ—namely, where's my place? We say with Isaiah, "Here am I. Send me" (Isaiah 6:8). We ask with Paul in Acts 22:10, "What would You have me to do, Lord?"

The Christian's whole life is in response to God's voice announcing Christ's lordship over all of life—every relationship, educational experience, and job. Once a Christian is secure in his or her identity in Christ, he or she is more likely to hear and fulfill God's call on his or her life. Such a Christian can then ask this central question: Where's my place? Or what would you have me to do? The individual makes his or her entire life an answer to this one question in the second season of spiritual formation, and the believer does so in order to stand strong in the Lord against all the other voices of the evil one and the world. As the Christian martyr Dietrich Bonhoeffer pondered as he wrote from a prison cell in Germany, "Who stands fast?" Bonhoeffer asserted, "Only the responsible man, who tries to make his whole life an answer to the question and call of God."[3]

The Christian man moves into God's world with confidence, knowing he is a glorious ruin redeemed to cultivate and transform culture, to plant his seed, to pursue a godly wife, perhaps, to multiply his life, and to know that every ordinary act of kindness in the place where God puts him counts for eternity. The former Dutch prime

---

[3] Dietrich Bonhoeffer, *Letters and Papers from Prison* (1953; repr. New York: The Macmillan Company, 1967), 4.

minister Abraham Kuyper, a former pastor, saw all culture's spheres under God's sovereign rule. He expressed it like this:

> There is not a single square inch of the entire creation about which Jesus Christ does not cry out, 'This is Mine! This belongs to Me!' We need to realize that our calling in terms of work is only one of our vocations. We are also called to be saints, parents, children, siblings, citizens, and a host of other things. These are truly vocations or callings.[4]

Christian women often find the central question about calling and finding their place difficult. Katelyn Beaty wrote in her excellent book *A Woman's Place: A Christian Vision for Your Calling in the Office, the Home, and the World*:

> We Christians have ways to talk about the joys of motherhood, and we should continue to do so. And certainly some women find returning to work as difficult as some women find leaving it. But we also need language to talk about joys of the kind that Andrea loves and misses. And when women voluntarily leave one kind of joy (paid work) for another (parenting), we need to recognize the loss as real, not as inherently selfish or careerist. We need to learn how to come alongside women who find the departure from work painful and even dehumanizing, because it is a departure from one profound way that they bear the image of God. If work is good and dignifying for men; if it is good

---

[4] Quote from Kuyper's inaugural address at the dedication of the Free University. Found in *Abraham Kuyper: A Centennial Reader*, ed. James D. Bratt (Grand Rapids, MI: Eerdmans, 1998), 488.

and dignifying for people in developing countries receiving microloans to start their own businesses; if it is good and dignifying for college graduates landing their first job— then work is good and dignifying for the stay-at-home mother with three kids. We would be remiss not to see that.[5]

Beaty also gives an example of the importance of a woman's calling through the life of Alice Seeley Harris. In 1870, the year Harris was born, Victorian England was enjoying unprecedented innovation, industry, and prosperity in every sector of society. Queen Victoria, as a woman, wielded authority on account of the royal throne, ruling over the largest empire the world. British culture, however, rested mostly on the power of men. Beaty explains:

> Pervasive in the Victorian era was the notion of "separate spheres." Women, it was believed, were naturally suited to oversee the spheres of home and family life, and men were naturally suited to oversee the spheres of economic activity and civic life. Even the queen affirmed separate spheres— although she clearly defied them! As she wrote in a letter in 1870, "God created men and women different— then let them remain each in their own position."

But Harris apparently was not restricted to the home when she married John Hobbis Harris in 1898. Before marrying, Alice worked at a London post office while training to be a missionary. A missionary was one of the few professions of the time that allowed women to travel the world, sometimes alone.

---

[5] Katelyn Beaty (2016-07-19). *A Woman's Place: A Christian Vision for Your Calling in the Office, the Home, and the World* (Kindle Locations 926-932). Howard Books. Kindle Edition.

The Harrises sailed to the Belgian Congo, a region in central Africa then controlled by King Leopold II of Belgium. Since 1885, Leopold had claimed the Congo Free State (CFS) as his personal property, ostensibly so that Christianity could take root in its basins and rain forests. Leopold, however, turned the CFS into a labor camp and exploited its natural resources. An estimated ten million innocent Congolese died in Leopold's camps.

When Alice and John arrived in the Belgian Congo, they were surprised by the cruelty of Belgian field officers. Here is how author Judy Pollard Smith imagines a significant encounter that deeply affected Alice. Smith wrote the following based on Alice's records:

> I could see that the young man at the front of the group was particularly devastated. His face was twisted in anguish. His friends led him forward by his elbows toward me ... The young man sank onto the porch and I thought he may collapse. He was carrying a small bundle bound about in plantain leaves ... I opened it with greater care than was usual because I was not sure what I was in for, given the way they looked at me with such burden etched on each face. To my own horror out fell two tiny pieces of human anatomy: a tiny child's foot, a tiny hand.[6]

Beaty wrote that the man Nsala had carried the remains of his five-year-old girl to the missionaries. Belgian officers had killed his child after Nsala failed to meet his quotas in the field.

Beaty explained that in response, Alice did something remarkable, brave, and even "unwomanly" for her time. She asked

---

[6] Judy Pollard Smith. *Don't Call Me Lady: The Journey of Lady Alice Seeley Harris* (Bloomington, IN: Abbott Press, 2014), 54.

Nsala to pose sitting on the veranda and looking down at the severed hand and foot of his child. Then she took a photograph using a portable Kodak camera, one of the first that could be loaded in daylight.

Even though Alice had no experience with photography, she began taking photos of other Congolese who had been mistreated. Then she sent the photos back to her host mission's agency as evidence of the violence in the field. Within five years, Alice's photos had circulated beyond the agency's magazine. The Harrises took the Harris Lantern Slide Show on tour throughout England and the United States to garner support for their antislavery society. Ordinary citizens who had assumed Leopold's rule was benevolent were given stark evidence of the carnage of colonialism.

Beaty notes that Mark Twain was profoundly affected by Alice's photos. In 1905, he wrote a satirical pamphlet in the voice of King Leopold: "The Kodak has been a sole calamity for us. The most powerful enemy indeed ... the only witness I couldn't bribe!" Some editions of King Leopold's soliloquy include reprints of Alice's photo of Nsala.

The campaign against Leopold's rule in the CFS became a global concern. By 1908, control of the Congo had finally fallen to the Belgian government. Beaty concludes:

> Alice didn't work alone; she joined a vast network of journalists, activists, and other missionaries laboring to ensure that Leopold's violence was on display for the world to see. But the power of her photographs is hard to protest. As one UK journalist notes, "The fact that Leopold lost his unfettered control so soon after Alice's photos were made widely available to the public in Europe tells

its own story." Today, Alice is remembered as the first photographer to campaign for human rights.[7]

Beaty added that Alice also raised four children.

Calling's Definition

Calling is more difficult to define than identity, and even harder to clarify with Bible verses because it is unique to each Christian. One ought not to get discouraged about discovering one's calling during this season of spiritual formation, for it is a dynamic process born through spiritual disciplines of solitude with God where God's Word and prayer work in conjunction with the Holy Spirit to shape and direct the Christian to fulfill the good works predestined beforehand by God (Ephesians 2:10). Calling formation is for a season, not a mere job decision that lasts a week or so. It usually takes from age eighteen to thirty-five, but is always renewing with changes in our particular callings within our general calling to Christ.

Calling is known by a process of trusting in the Lord's leading by knowing of your holy longings and by interpreting your life's story according to the gospel narrative of scripture. We gain a sense of our calling to Christ as we obey the Lord in the context of our Christian community where our spiritual gifts and experiences are known in one particular place. It may be a "Nazareth" where you will impact the world by remaining identified with it. Jesus reached the world by living within the limitations of one place and people in history. He was known as "Jesus of Nazareth" from childhood to death. Above sacred head on the cross it read, "Jesus of Nazareth." Paul, "Saul of Tarsus," took some time after his conversion and initial call

---

[7] Beaty, Katelyn (2016-07-19). *A Woman's Place: A Christian Vision for Your Calling in the Office, the Home, and the World* (New York, NY: Howard Books, 2016), Kindle Locations 391-398.

from Christ was announced. The first disciples (Galileans) grew to gain their sense of callings, too, which grew over the years by being with Jesus before crucifixion and after resurrection. They served in particular places, sometimes pursued their pre-vocations, were married or not, and all were called to be martyrs for Christ.

This explains why the calling question gets neglected in a culture that insists like a rationalist that it be immediately certain of his goal or it is not worth pursuing. Also, the general impatience with trusting God is rare in a culture that also has been influenced by irrationalism—dismissing truth altogether. Christian calling, however, is the truth that God calls us to self first of all in order to discover how meaningful all of life is to Christians wherever God places them. This is how Os Guiness defined calling:

> Calling is the truth that God calls us to Himself so decisively that everything we are, everything we do, and everything we have is invested with a special devotion, dynamism, and direction lived out as a response to summons and service.[8]

The ancients used the term *Coram Deo*, which translates, "To live in one world before the face of God." God's face is toward you to speak blessings and benedictions (good words about your future) over every area of your life. The notion of calling comes from the fact that God communicates to people; He speaks to us through His word and providence. He calls us each by name, which is engraved on the palms of His hands and written in heaven. Vocation comes from the Latin root *vox* or *voco* (verbal orders of the commanding officer). A vocation is not merely one's choice of career or a decision to get married, but is a matter of hearing a higher call or voice from God

---

[8] Os Guinness, *The Call: Finding and Fulfilling the Central Purpose of Your Life* (Nashville, TN: Word Publishing, 1998), p. 29.

when we make such decisions. Calling comes from outside of us, and we can use our "insides" to hear His call in the context of solitude where and when we meet with God face to face (See Appendix).

Calling's Extensiveness: All of Life

Calling invests and shapes our employment, discipleship, and church membership. It gives devotion to our stewardship of creation and to every gift God gives you. Calling brings clarity to all our relationships in order to clarify whether to be single or married, to parent or not, and how to live as a son or a daughter for your parent(s)' honor.

A job, a marriage, singleness, or a ministry may all be identified as particular callings of ours within our common overall general calling. This is why Henri Nouwen said marriage is a particular calling itself to Christ, similar to Paul's words in 1 Corinthians 7. Nouwen wrote:

> Marriage is foremost a vocation. Two people are called together to fulfill a mission that God has given them. Marriage is a spiritual reality. That is to say, a man and a woman come together for life, not just because they experience deep love for each other, but because they believe that God loves each of them with an infinite love and has called them to each other to be living witnesses of that love. To love is to embody God's infinite love in a faithful communion with another human being.[9]

---

[9] Henri J. M.; Nouwen, *Here and Now: Living in the Spirit* (Danvers, MA: The Crossroad Publishing Company, 1994), Kindle Locations 1275-1278. Kindle Edition.

My wife, Karen, has been called into a variety of particular roles and places. She was called to Christ first and foremost, which led to particular calls to honor parents, to marry, to raise five children, to nurture eleven grandchildren, to invest her life into faithful women through discipleship, to counsel sexually abused women, to serve as a pastor's wife, to educate children in three school systems—home, public, and private Christian. Her calling portfolio has variety and changes, but only becomes clearer as she abides in Christ. These and other good works were predestined for her to walk into (Ephesians 2:10).

Karen sensed a call to teach at Cornerstone Christian Academy in Bloomington, Illinois, where we live. We prayed, and her inward sense of call was matched by the outward call issued from the school. This constitutes a call; namely, when one's inward longing to serve people in a place and way is confirmed by the outward call to serve by those very people in authority. After ten years or so, however, she recently began to own a heart to create wealth through EBay at home. As she sensed God was releasing her from her work at the school, she also sensed a strong desire to work in her home and enjoy retail. She loves her new job and is more flexible to visit and invest in her grandchildren and other ministries at church.

Our calling to Christ is extensive because it involves all of life.

Calling's Clarification: My Life's Purpose

One of the sad facts of modern culture is the loss of purpose for living. In fact, the college students of today are often unable to identify any purpose behind their major field of study besides getting a job that earns money. One of the main sorrows I experienced in college that brought me to Christ was my lack of purpose for living, for college, a job, and a future. Even Christians are often confused about how their parachurch ministry experience equipped them in college years to value their education or vocational pursuits.

Christians must revive the doctrine of calling for two reasons. We may be easily influenced by the notion that there is no purpose in life, and we can offer hope to those outside the faith who struggle with a sense of meaninglessness in everyday life. Os Guiness mentions three factors for why the question of calling is so urgently needed. He writes:

> In our own day this question is urgent in the highly modern parts of the world, and there is a simple reason why. Three factors have converged to fuel a search for significance without precedent in human history. First, the search for purpose of life is one of the deepest issues of our experiences as human beings. Second, the expectation that we can all live purposeful lives has been given a gigantic boost by modern society's offer to maximum opportunity for choice and change in all we do. Third, fulfillment of the search for purpose is thwarted by a stunning fact: Out of more than a score of great civilizations in human history, modern Western civilization is the very first to have no agreed-on answer to the question of the purpose of life. Thus more ignorance, confusion—and longing—surround this topic now than at almost any time in history. The trouble is that, as modern people, we have too much to live with and too little to live for. Some feel they have time but not enough money; others feel they have

money but not enough time. But for most of us, in the midst of plenty, we have spiritual poverty.[10]

Take heart as you read each chapter. Chapter 3 will challenge the reader because it addresses eight hindrances to calling. These hindrances must be removed in order to clearly sense God's calling for your life. Although this may be a painful process, I pray it is for each reader a sorrow unto life (2 Corinthians 7:11). Press on. You won't regret it because there are good results ahead. Here are three benefits you can anticipate as a result of discerning your calling to Christ

One, your calling will subvert the idols of choice and frenetic busyness in our culture. Two, your calling will provide a gospel storyline and unity rather than a fragmented disconnection of relationships, events, and places. Three, your growing sense of calling to Christ will make you single-minded and increase your effectiveness in more areas. "This one thing I do," said the apostle doing so many things. His calling to Christ was the clearest motivation for him, but he fulfilled it in a thousand ways.

As we seek to understand the doctrine of calling, we noted that it begins with a heart transformed by the power of the Holy Spirit in response to God's grace and gospel before we seek it. As the Christian reaches adulthood, he or she asks God an important question; namely, where's my place?

Having given definition to what is meant by Christian calling, we see its depth in a way that teaches us to be patient in the process to discover it. We also addressed its extensiveness—how it touches every aspect of our lives. Before we make it too practical at this point, we need a more solid theological foundation and understanding that

---

[10] Os Guiness, *The Call: Finding and Fulfilling the Central Purpose of Your Life* (Nashville, TN: Word Publishing, 1998), pp. 2–3.

will lead to a better discovery of our unique and personal experience and practice. This is the subject of the next chapter.

Thoughts for Group Leaders

Two instructions:

1. Take time at the first meeting to introduce yourselves and share answers to this question: What do you hope to gain from this group and book?
2. Show them the last chapter's template so the members may understand that the aim is to share what we sense our calling to Christ is with one another at the end of the book.

Three considerations for the leader:

1. Our generation needs spiritual formation leaders like you, who are willing to shape believers from broken and crippled conformists into creative and free transformational agents of grace. Our generation needs spiritual formation leaders like you, who are willing to equip others to discern crippling voices from Christ's voice so they may become creatively free and transformational agents of grace.
2. Your heart matters. A heart filled with faith, hope, and love will make all the difference in your members' lives. Faith asks, "What am I trusting God for in each person's calling?" Hope ponders, "What's my vision for this person in five and ten years from now?" Finally, love desires to see each person blossom in the Lord's vineyard where he has chosen to plant him or her.

3. Environment—As you share your own brokenness, you will give your group members permission to do the same. Thus, you'll create an environment of grace, a safe place for people to come to terms with the broken people they truly are, responding to Christ's calling of glory they hope to become. Emphasize confidentiality from the start.

Group Discussion Questions:

1. What is the Christian's calling question? Have you asked God this in prayer? When? What happened?
2. Do you see the connection of the four seasons of spiritual formation? Why is it important to study identity in Christ before calling to Christ? Do you think that without a clear sense of identity in Christ and calling to Christ, the Christian is likely to become less intentional for Christ and less clear about his legacy from Christ?
3. Do you believe people lack purpose for living in contemporary culture? How would a sense of calling invest peoples' lives with a special devotion, dynamism, and direction?

Chapter 2
The Scriptural and Theological Basis of Calling

General and Particular Callings

Although the word *kaleo* used for "calling" means God's general summons to us, it is may be applied in all areas of life. God summons us to repent and believe in Christ (1 Corinthians. 1:9; Romans. 8:30); to fulfill the Great Commission (1 Peter 2:9–10); and to join in a local church of "called out ones" *(ekklesia)*. God calls each Christian to a general calling and to particular callings, which includes all of life— our gifts, story, family status, employment, and regular responsibilities in God's world.

It may be helpful, therefore, to differentiate the Christian calling into two categories; namely, our general calling to Christ and our particular callings to Christ. Our general calling comes from God to every Christian, but our particular callings vary from one Christian to another. Our particular callings put us within the limitations of relationships and places that we may serve Christ there by serving people for longer times. Concerning where people live, Paul asserted, "[God] determined allotted periods and boundaries of their dwelling place" (Acts 17:26). Just as God has a purpose for the places we serve Him, He has people there receiving our services. As the Puritan

William Perkins wrote, "The main purpose of our lives is to serve God by serving men, in our callings."[11]

When we experience the power of God's effectual call on our lives (general calling), it is so transformational that we may assume God no longer wants us to remain in our particular callings. Does our transformational experience of being called out of darkness into light mean that God is calling us out of the ordinary relationships, places, and jobs into a different relational status, like Paul's to work full-time ministry? We may assume that God, in the main, wants us to remain in our particular callings when we are converted. The truth is that God rarely counsels us in scripture to undo or change our particular callings in light of the general calling.

In 1 Corinthians 7:17, Christians were taught that it was unnecessary to change what they were currently doing in life after their experience of conversion. "Only let each person lead the life that the Lord has *assigned* to him, and to which God has *called* him. This is my rule in all the churches." God has already called us into particular callings before our conversion. "Assigned" and "called" are two significantly weighted words that imply that God equips us with various talents and gifts for building up the greater community He placed us in and outside the local church—in the culture at large. We are called by God to love in the context of community before we may be called as a Christian. We have work and services assigned to us by God, which provides purpose to our common work and ordinary places of day-to-day effort.

---

[11] William Perkins's *A Treatise of the Vocations or Callings of Men* is quoted in Os Guiness, *The Call: Finding and Fulfilling the Central Purpose of Your Life* (Nashville, TN: Word Publishing, 1998), p. 35.

Demolishing the Dividing Wall: The Sacred/Secular Split

> A sense of God's calling us to work and serve in all of life, of course, breaks down the artificial wall Western culture has erected in order to make a divide between the secular and the sacred. In the Christian worldview there is no place or aspect of culture that is "secular." All is sacred in the sense that Jesus is Lord over all (God is transcendent); all is done through Him (God is omnipresent); and He is in all (God is immanent). When Christians make a divide between sacred and secular callings, they deny the scripture's teaching, language, and joyful experience that our callings to Christ are furnished with.[12]

One of the recoveries from the Reformation after the darkness of the Middle Ages was the truth that every Christian's calling is sacred, whether you serve in full-time vocational ministry or serve in a factory, for a school, or on a farm. The reformer Martin Luther made the doctrine of calling to Christ plain to understand by putting it this way:

> [T]he works of monks and priests, however holy and arduous they might be, do not differ one whit in the sight of God from the works of the rustic laborer in the field or the woman going about her household task. But all works are measured before God by faith alone. Indeed the menial labor of a manservant or a

---

[12] This is Francis Schaeffer's emphasis in his writings. *The Complete Works of Francis A. Schaeffer: A Christian Worldview* (Wheaton, IL: Crossway Books, 1982), Five volumes.

maidservant is often more acceptable to God than all the fastings of a monk or a priest because the monk or priest lacks faith.[13]

So then, the Christian has a general calling and particular callings, which all matter in our relationship to Christ. The Christian's calling to Christ is sacred to God because Christ cares about all of creation and culture, not just one hour of church on Sundays.

One of my sons, Nate, aced all his seminary classes. He believed God had called to become a Christian pastor for a number of years. In order to get through seminary, he used what he thought was a pre-vocational calling in chemistry. As he came to the end of seminary, however, he realized that chemistry was his primary vocation. He courageously announced his decision to leave seminary training and went full time working as a chemist for Christ. In the moment, I was surprised by his decision because it changed after many years of seeking full-time vocational service in Christian ministry, but I am so thankful that he settled his sense of calling now. His joy in chemistry is evident to all, and chemistry is a sacred calling.

God Calls us to Work

The Bible begins with what is most important for us to make sense of God's world. God reveals Himself, His world, our identity in Christ, and our callings to Christ. Spiritual formation begins with biblical theology and a Christian worldview in the very first seasons of identity and calling. God explains not only who we are, but He also describes particular callings designed for us to work in His creation. God called Adam into the garden to produce and provide, and into marriage to protect and to delight in Eve, and into

---

[13] Martin Luther, *The Babylonian Captivity of the Church* (1520).

fatherhood to equip another generation of workers (Genesis 2:7–8, 15–25; 4:1–2).

Work was initially established not in the cursed and groaning soil of life, but in the blessed soil of the garden of Eden. Our work, like food, sexual pleasure in marriage, rest, and prayer were a regular part of life before the fall. Our particular callings were in place before the fall of humanity and our conversion, and they remain afterwards.

Our work is connected to God's work; even in the way we number the days of the workweek to rest from our work on the Lord's Day. We are made to enjoy our work and to stand back and declare: "My work has eternal worth." The Bible begins with God at work and God at rest. It begins with humanity at work and humanity at rest in the same rhythms God had ordained for us to enjoy each day, week, and year. This remains, because Christ has redeemed all things that were originally ordered and then complicated by the fall. The implication is that our particular callings from God to work hard and to create wealth are not to be viewed as necessary evils. Rather, we learn that Adam and Eve were designed to work as God works out of sheer joy, and to look back on a week's work with inward rest and name it good.

God is into the ordinary work of our particular callings

God made the world as an artist or craftsman creates a masterpiece. We were made in God's image, and put in His garden to do ordinary work in creative and joyful ways. The word for God at *work* is *mlkh*, which is the word for ordinary human work. The Bible teaches us that we ought to aspire to live ordinary lives with eternal consequences for the glory of Christ. The apostolic message from Paul in the context of waiting for Christ's return is for Christians to "aspire to live quietly, and to mind your own affairs, and to work with your hands, as we instructed you, so that you may walk properly before outsiders and be dependent on no one" (1 Thessalonians 4:11–12).

Christians, like those in Thessalonica who were focused on Christ's imminent return, have lost interest in quiet living, minding their affairs, and working because these seem unimportant in light of eternal life. This is the wrong approach to living in the light of eternity. What would you do if Christ were to return tomorrow? I hope you would say you would plant a tree or invest in others by serving them and not say that you would choose some form of escaping your calling.

Avocations, which are minor jobs or hobbies, are within the portfolio of a Christian's overall and general calling. God is into everything lawful, edifying, profitable, and beneficial to others. When we exercise or invest in music and the arts, we sense God's pleasure. Even our difficult pre-vocations, which are temporary employments and first opportunities to work, are part of our overall calling to Christ.

I worked in the steel mills of Gary, Indiana, during the summers while attending Purdue University for four years. I would leave my beautiful hometown of Ogden Dunes along Lake Michigan with sand dunes, beautiful woods, and beach life in order to drive into the polluted, productive steel mills to work. I wore a yellow helmet, protective goggles, special dark-green clothing, and steel-tipped boots. It was like serving for the armed forces in a war zone. I watched hot steel made from a liquid in furnaces where the workers wore metal-looking astronaut suits. The language was rough, and the culture was politically incorrect according to today's standards. They knew college students were temporary workers. It was my pre-vocational summer job. Their vocational work mattered.

They called us "summertime." "Hey, summertime," they'd call out to us, "dig this sludge out." We had the worst tasks imaginable at times, and we would say to each other, "I'm definitely finishing college so I never have to work here." When I drove out of the parking lot, there was a car-washing process to take off the falling soot from the cars. Before I showered at home, I used industrial soap to take the black grime from my hands.

Now, what does that pre-vocational job of affliction have to do with my overall calling to Christ, and my particular calling to serve as a gospel preacher and senior pastor? Well, it was there I learned to respect people serving in jobs that others benefit from. It was there that someone first shared the gospel with me, though I wasn't ready to receive it. I learned about other cultures of all kinds that I had not known well until then. I came to appreciate all the trades that go into making steel, and I can trust that God was shaping my character and preparing me in the furnace of affliction for working even harder in the furnace of full-time ministry.

God is behind our pre-vocations because he is behind our vocations. He puts on our heart our pre-vocations and avocations because they are on his heart too. Working jobs to get through schooling is an aspect of shaping us for a future vocation. Joseph served under his parents, a government official, and a prison guard before he served under the king. David served as a shepherd to prepare him to serve as a warrior and a king to shepherd God's people. John, James, and Peter served as fishermen before they were fishers of men (Matthew 4:19). Paul was a theological student and scholar, also a tent maker, before he was an apostle to the nations and a gospel theologian. Luke was a physician before and while he was serving as a missionary and sacred historian. We can trust that God purposefully designs every aspect of our overall general calling to Christ, and gives us particular callings that are often fashioned in the furnaces, factories, and classrooms of affliction.

In fact, God has so much to say in the Bible about working, serving, and employment that it is a wonder how Christians made this major chunk of our lives seem so unimportant and "secular" in the sight and presence of God throughout the week! Just as the Greeks viewed manual labor as demeaning, Christendom in the Medieval period viewed it as "secular" work, as less valuable to Christ than work in and for the Church. This is why Martin Luther attacked this false notion effectively in his treatise *To the Christian Nobility of the German Nation:*

> It is pure invention [fiction] that Pope, bishops, priests, and monks are called "spiritual estate" while princes, lords, artisans, and farmers are called the "temporal estate." This is indeed a piece of deceit and hypocrisy ... Yet no one need be intimidated by it, and that for this reason: all Christians are truly of the spiritual estate, and there is no difference among them except that of office ... We are all consecrated priests.[14]

The Reformers' understanding of how sacred and important our work is to Christ ignited the laity to work as to the Lord, rather than to please men (Colossians 3:23–24). By the twentieth century, however, many Protestant churches were silent about this issue. In that period Dorothy Sayers questioned why the Church was rarely addressing how one's work matters to God, and why preachers rarely use the Bible's many passages to do so. In her essay, "Why Work?" in *Creed or Chaos* she complains:

> The church's approach to an intelligent carpenter is usually confined to exhorting him to not be drunk and disorderly in his leisure hours and to come to church on Sundays. What the church should be

---

[14] Martin Luther, *Three Treatises* (Philadelphia, PA: Fortress Press, 1970), p. 12.

telling him is this: that the very first demand that his religion makes upon him is that he should make good tables.[15]

It seems that even our identity is shaped by our callings, and somewhat closely related. Our names receive prefixes like "Mrs." or "Dr.," and we are asked what we do when introducing ourselves to new people. Our callings, which involve work, is what we live to do. Therefore, it is vital that we value our work because God cares about what we are living for. Sayers concluded:

> What is the Christian understanding of work? ... [It] is that work is not, primarily, a thing one does to live, but the thing one lives to do. It is, or it should be, the full expression of the worker's faculties ... the medium in which he offers himself to God.[16]

She was attacking the modern world's notion that work is simply about earning money, which was becoming predominant in the minds of the British in the 1940s:

> I believe there is a Christian doctrine of work, very closely related to the doctrines of the creative energy of God and the divine image in man ... The essential heresy ... being that work is not the expression of man's creative energy in service of Society, but only something one does in order to obtain money and leisure.[17]

---

[15] Dorothy Sayers, *Creed or Chaos* (New York, NY: Harcourt, Brace, 1949), p. 51.
[16] *Ibid.*, p. 53.
[17] *Ibid.*, pp. 42–43. See also, Timothy Keller, "Vocation: Discerning Your Calling," www.redeemercitytocity.com

God is calling us to fulfill His works through our good works (Psalm 127:1). William Perkins wrote: "A vocation or calling is a certain kind of life, ordained and imposed on man by God for the common good."[18] He is building the house through us. In the Old Testament, God cared about the craftsmen, not just the work of the priests. God first sent the Holy Spirit upon craftsmen in the Old Testament (Exodus 28:3; 31:1–5). God is working behind all our deeds in a thousand places because he is hiding through us to serve others in ordinary acts of kindness and justice. Martin Luther wrote:

> What else is all our work to God—whether in the fields, in the garden, in the city, in the house, in war, or in government—but just such a child's performance, by which He wants to give His gifts in the fields, at home, and everywhere else? These are the masks of God, behind which He wants to remain concealed and do all things.[19]

God planned your good works and calling.

Our good works are planned by Him in eternity, but lived out by us on earth. (Ephesians 2:10) They are God's gracious privileges for us to enjoy as new creations in Christ. We were saved by grace to live to Christ by grace in all of life. God creates and cares for everything, and then calls workers to labor in it and to keep it (Genesis 1–2). His command to "fill the earth and subdue it" implies that there is a lot more for us to fulfill through our particular callings.

When God called us to "subdue the earth" He gave humanity the cultural mandate to act as His trustees with creation under our

---

[18] William Perkins, *A Treatise of the Vocations* is copied in William C. Placher, editor, *Callings: Twenty Centuries of Christian Wisdom on Vocation* (Grand Rapids, MI: Eerdmans Publishing Company, 2005), p. 262.

[19] Jaroslav Pelikan, editor, *Luther's Works* (St. Louis, MO: Concordia Publishing House, 1955), Volume 14, p. 96.

care to cultivate it. It requires a childlike willfulness on our part to our heavenly Father. Tim Keller of Redeemer Presbyterian puts it like this:

> Whenever we bring order out of chaos, whenever we draw out creative potential, whenever we elaborate and "unfold" creation beyond where it was when we found it, we are following God's pattern of creative cultural development. In fact, our word "culture" comes from this idea of cultivation. Just as he subdued the earth in his work of creation, so he calls us now to labor as his representatives in a continuation and extension of that work of subduing.[20]

Nehemiah's Calling

Nehemiah calling was to bring order out of chaos when he was commissioned to rebuild the walls broken down in Jerusalem during the exile of God's people. He petitioned the king for the job because God burdened him to the point of tears to see the restoration project completed.

> As soon as I heard these words I sat down and wept and mourned for days, and I continued fasting and praying before the God of heaven. (Nehemiah 1:4)

Nehemiah immediately sensed God's inward call, and the outward call came from the king himself. The king released Nehemiah from his job as a cupbearer to the king to become a construction site manager over the remnant of Israel for the King of heaven. He wrote:

---

[20] Timothy Keller, *Every Good Endeavor: Connecting Your Work to God's Work* (New York, NY: Dutton, 2012), p. 59.

"And the king granted me what I asked, for the good hand of my God was upon me" (Nehemiah 2:8).

The account of Nehemiah is very beneficial for us to consider our work in the kind of culture we have in the Western world because it starts for Nehemiah with a boss who is a nonbeliever and meets with resistance from outsiders at the job site.

Sanballat, Tobia, and others are angry when they hear about the building of the wall (Nehemiah 4:1). As they taunt Nehemiah and his staff, we learn about how to overcome resistance and trials at our places of work.

Overcoming Opposition in Our Callings

Nehemiah's sense of calling is the foundation for overcoming opposition to our work, which we believe God assigned to us in order to finish for Christ's glory. We learn three lessons about this through Nehemiah's faithfulness to the Lord.

The first lesson is this: Since God called us and assigned us to our workplaces, we ought to pray for God's support when we meet opposition. Nehemiah simply prays: "Hear, O our God, for we are despised. Turn back their taunt on their own heads … for they have provoked You to anger in the presence of the builders" (Nehemiah 4:4–5). Since God called you to work in your place of employment, you can be sure that He will support you when you ask for His help. Nehemiah encouraged his fellow believers at work

> Do not be afraid of them. Remember the Lord, who is great and awesome, and fight for your brothers, your sons, your daughters, your wives, and your homes. (Nehemiah 4:14)

Although the work stopped for a time, God heard their prayers and the work resumed.

The second lesson is this: God is always at work in the work he calls you to do. "Our God," declared Nehemiah, "will fight for us" (Nehemiah 4:20). God, who is always at work, says to humanity through Adam in the garden's dirt to "work it and keep it" (Genesis 2:15). Jesus declared: "My Father is always at His work to this very day, and I too am working" (John 5:17). We, too, are working, but never alone because God is working in and through us for His own purposes.

One way we know that God is always at work still is that people are the work of His hands. You are a wonderful work of God! God is still at work in the wombs of mothers. His work in making you in your mother's womb and later as a new creation is praiseworthy. "I praise you because I am fearfully and wonderfully made. Wonderful are your works; my soul knows it full well" (Psalm 139:13–16; Ephesians 2:10).

God calls us to work with Him today and to enjoy creating wealth and providing services to others. He is hiding in us, and He wants us to ask for that very confirmation. Listen to what He says to us through the prophet: "I am the Lord who teaches you to profit" (Isaiah 48:17–18). Follow the example of the psalmist, Moses, by praying: "Let the favor of the Lord our God be upon us, and establish the work of our hands upon us; yes, establish the work of our hands" (Psalm 90:17). Nehemiah and his workers were able to stop the oppression of the poor through their work because God is always at work in this way as well (Nehemiah 5).

The third lesson from Nehemiah about opposition at work, God's work, is this: since it is God's assignment and work, you don't have to pay attention to every opposing word or invitation to engage in a fight. When Sanballat and another wanted to meet with Nehemiah, Nehemiah replied: "I am doing a great work and I cannot come down, Why should the work stop while I leave it and come down with you?" This invitation to bicker was refused four times by Nehemiah in the same manner (Nehemiah 6:3–4). Does opposition rule you? Do your critics set your agenda and rule your thoughts?

The fifth time Sanballat sent an accusatory letter, and Nehemiah's reply was short and to the point. The reply read: "No such things as you say have been done, for you are inventing them out of your own mind" (Nehemiah 6:8). You can refuse invitations to fight, and sometimes simply refuse their words outright.

Finally, we learn the fourth lesson; namely, that God will vindicate you and the work done in His Name and for His glory in the end. Nehemiah put it this way:

> So the wall was finished … in fifty-two days. And when all our enemies heard of it, all the nations around were afraid and fell greatly in their own esteem, for they perceived that this work had been accomplished with the help of our God. (Nehemiah 6:15–16)

God is for you in your workplace because He put you there. Your work matters to God, so you can pray for help in moments of unfair opposition. When you meet with resistance, remember God is meeting resistance in His work. Thankfully, you are not required to come to the repeated invitations of those wanting to fight with you, and you can sometimes tell it to them straight. In the end, know this: God is glorified in vindicating His children.

The Bible provides us a theology of calling that makes our work meaningful. Since you are a work of God prepared for good works and He is working through your efforts, you may view your works as a privilege to image God in all your grand endeavors.

Group Discussion Questions:

1. Do you work to live or live to work?
2. How have your pre-vocations shaped you? How did God use them to prepare you for your primary vocation?
3. How has the sacred-secular dividing wall of Western culture made large parts of culture and life less meaningful for you in relation to Christ?
4. If you wrote out your portfolio of particular callings that comprise your overall and general calling to Christ, what would they include? For example, God may have particular callings on your life to be a son or a daughter, husband or wife, parent or grandparent, full-time or part-time employee, officer or leader in your church, etc.
5. Does you work seem rather ordinary?
6. Do you ever doubt that your work has significance in the Christian life? Did you have any thoughts to share regarding the quote from Martin Luther: "All Christians are of the same spiritual estate?"
7. How does a sense of calling invest your work with purpose and significance?
8. What is the Christian understanding of work? "What should the Church tell the carpenter? Make good tables?" (Dorothy Sayers)
9. How was your experience in practicing the spiritual discipline of solitude this week?

Ten Questions for the Spiritual Discipline of Solitude this week:

1. Am I okay with being in a garden to work with my spouse and children or as an unmarried adult without children? Is

that enough? Is that spiritual enough? See Genesis 2 and 1 Thessalonians 4:11–12.
2. How do I see my work as more than a "necessary evil," and more of a call to serve Christ wholeheartedly? See Colossians 3:23–24.
3. Do I rest from my principal vocation well, while looking back and calling it good? See Ecclesiastes 2:24; 3:12–13.
4. How has God used "pre-vocations" in my life?
5. How is God at work in my work?
6. Am I excited about future work God has for me?
7. I am God's workmanship (*poema*) created to fulfill good works He has planned. How does that give me hope today?
8. What is God calling me to subdue this week by bringing order out of chaos and drawing out my creative potential?
9. How can I be of greatest service to other people, knowing that what I do matters in serving human needs?
10. How does God want me to create wealth? Ask for His wisdom and for confirmation upon the work of your hands this week.

Chapter 3
Eight Hindrances to Joy in One's Calling

Although we may encounter resistance from the outside in our callings, much of the opposition to our joy is related to internal hindrances in our own hearts. A *hindrance* is something that causes resistance, delay, or obstruction to a development process. It is an obstacle, a handicap, a restriction, and an interference in your experience and calling. Here are eight common hindrances to joy in one's calling.

Idolatry

The first hindrance to fulfilling our calling to Christ is idolatry. John Calvin commented on how human nature is a perpetual forge or factory of idols.[21] How does idolatry shape our calling and work? Idolatry happens in us whenever we refuse to believe the gospel, that God is pleased with us, and then proceed to get God to love us through our callings. In his *Treatise Concerning Good Works*, Luther wrote:

---

[21] John Calvin, *Institutes of the Christian Religion* (Philadelphia, PA: The Westminster Press, 1960), Volume One, p. 108. Book 1, Part 11, Section 8.

> The First Commandment commands: 'Thou shalt have no other gods,' which means: 'Since I alone am God. Thou shalt place all thy confidence trust and faith on Me alone, and on no one else.' ... All those who do not at all times trust God and ... His favor, grace and goodwill, but seek His favor in other things or in themselves, do not keep this Commandment, and practice real idolatry ... If we do not believe that God is gracious to us and is pleased with us, or if we presumptuously expect to please Him only through and after our works, then it is all pure deception, outwardly honoring God, but inwardly setting up self as a false god.[22]

What idols hinder your joy in your calling? Ask yourself these simple questions: Am I ruled by the idol of comfort? Do I work to fulfill my employer's mission, or only to take the employee benefits? Am I ruled by the idol of human approval? Paul warns against working hard only when the supervisor is watching. Rather than working "with a sincere heart, as you would Christ," Christians fall into the idolatry of "eye-service, as people-pleasers" (Ephesians 6:5–7). Am I trying to control the employees God gave me to supervise by threatening them or showing partiality (Ephesians 6:9)? Am I ruled by the idol of performance, which bases my acceptance with God on my performance rather than Christ's righteousness?[23] All these questions answered in the affirmative expose that we have made an idol out of our work, our supervisors, our position as a supervisor, or our performance. Is your identity in Christ, or merely

---

[22] Martin Luther, *Luther's Works*, Volume 44, p. 30.
[23] See Robert Davis Smart, *Identity in Christ: Renouncing Lies and Foolish Strategies* (Bloomington, IN: Westbow Press, 2017).

in your professional status? David Martyn Lloyd-Jones mentioned how sad it is when a Christian is ruled by the idol of professionalism:

[T]here are many whom I have had the privilege of meeting whose tombstones might well bear the grim epitaph "born a man, died a doctor!"[24]

Are you ruled by the idol of perfectionism? Perfectionism demands that your work must be flawless, or you will fall apart with an inordinate anger toward yourself or others.

Embracing the Sorrow

The simplest way to understand idolatry is to ask ourselves if we are ruled by our own desires. Desires are not the idols of your heart until they become demands. Simply put, a desire that is turned into a demand is an idol. Driving in late to work because of a traffic accident ahead confronts us with the choice to either embrace the sorrow of an unmet longing to make it on time or to be ruled by the "be-on-time-god." Whenever anxiety or anger shows up as a red warning sign on the dashboard of your heart, you must lift up the hood of your heart and ask yourself: what do I long for? If it is to be on time, then it is a legitimate longing. When anxiety and anger arise in your heart, however, about being on time, then your desire has become a demand. A desire that is made into a demand is always an idol of the heart because it exposes that you are trying to control what you cannot. Sure, you can be more responsible to be on time, but often other circumstances will block your goals. Unless you embrace the sorrow of being late and trust God's providence, you will be ruled by your own demands.

When I was a young pastor we had one van for a family of seven. I wanted to get to church on time, but "the be-on-time-god" was the

---

[24] David Martyn Lloyd-Jones, *Healing and the Scriptures* (Thomas Nelson, 1982), p. 14.

idol in my heart. I would hustle to get the kids ready for church while Karen would put eye makeup on in the bathroom mirror. As anxiety grew within, so did anger. I knew this because sarcasm is a form of anger, and I called Karen *Speed*. I would call up to her: "Hey, Speed! We'll be waiting in the van." When she came down into the van, she would pull the visor down to continue the beautification process. Inside my heart was anxiety and anger, but I wanted to maintain the image of a nice and godly pastor. If we made it on time, "be-on-time-god" would never love or reward me. He would say, "Huh, you barely made it." If we were late, then he heaped on the condemnation. Of course, the devil loves to accuse and condemn Christians, who allow him a foothold through idolatry.

Then one day I repented. I confessed to Karen that I made the "be-on-time-god" my god on Sunday mornings. I said to her, "I repent of this demand on you and my sarcasm. I am not going to allow evil in this home, or let it negatively affect our children." I explained my longing to be on time for church, and she agreed that it was legitimate. I asked for forgiveness, and she did too for being late. The main thing was that I was going to be a gospel lover. If she was late, then I said I would simply embrace the sorrow.

Guess what? Karen was motivated by grace, and not by my demand to be on time. She began to be on time more often, but she still would come into the van late sometimes. On those occasions she would pull down the visor with her tongue poking out to put on eyelash stuff, and say to me with a smile, "I know you're embracing the sorrow." We would laugh at ourselves over this, and do you know what? No one seemed to notice we were late because all the other people were stressed out as well, trying to make it on time.

Take time to remove the first major hindrance to joy in your calling to Christ by repentance; namely, removing the idols of your heart. Learn to "embrace the sorrow" of unmet longings instead of being filled with anxiety and anger.

Unhealthy Competition

The second major hindrance to joy in one's calling to Christ that we will address is unhealthy competition. Unholy competition is closely associated with pride and envy. C. S. Lewis in *Mere Christianity* describes this:

> Now what I want you to get clear is that Pride is essentially competitive—is competitive by its very nature ... Pride gets no pleasure out of having something, only out of having more of it than the next man. We say people are proud of being rich, or clever, or good-looking but they are not. They are proud of being richer, or cleverer, or better-looking than others.[25]

We are exhorted to have nothing to do with "rivalry or vain conceit" (Philippians 1:15, 2:3). Often this is a more common hindrance among the young, whose selfish ambition is for being in the in-crowd and among the "cool kids" at school and work. When the young and best were close to graduation in England, C. S. Lewis courageously challenged the graduates to "break" working to get into what he called "the inner ring" before it would "break" them. Lewis said:

> The quest of the Inner Ring will break your hearts unless you break it. But if you break it, a surprising result will follow. If in your working hours you make the work your end, you will presently find yourself all unawares inside the only circle in your profession that really matters. You will be one of the

---

[25] C. S. Lewis, *Mere Christianity* (San Francisco, CA: Harper, 2001), p. 122.

sound craftsmen, and other sound craftsmen will know it. This group of craftsmen will by no means coincide with the Inner Ring or the Important People or the People in the Know. It will not shape that professional policy or work up that professional influence which fights for the profession as a whole against the public: nor will it lead to those periodic scandals and crises, which the Inner Ring produces. But it will do those things, which that profession exists to do and will in the long run be responsible for all the respect which that profession in fact enjoys and which the speeches and advertisements cannot maintain. And if in your spare time you consort simply with the people you like, you will again find that you have come unawares to a real inside: that you are indeed snug and safe at the centre of something which, seen from without, would look exactly like an Inner Ring. But the difference is that the secrecy is accidental, and its exclusiveness a by-product, and no one was led thither by the lure of the esoteric: for it is only four or five people who like one another meeting to do things that they like. This is friendship. Aristotle placed it among the virtues. It causes perhaps half of all the happiness in the world, and no Inner Ring can ever have it. We are told in Scripture that those who ask get. That is true, in senses I can't now explore. But in another sense there is much truth in the schoolboy's principle "them as asks shan't have." To a young person, just entering on adult life, the world seems full of "insides," full of delightful intimacies and confidentialities, and he desires to enter them. But if he follows that desire he will reach no "inside" that is worth reaching.[26]

Just as idolatry and unholy competition can hinder our joy in our calling to Christ, our old default mode of our sinful natures hinder us as well.

Autonomous and Foolish Strategies

Thirdly, our default mode or natural way of living most be put off or put to death. We must give pause to its urges and compulsive responses to the circumstances we face each moment. In other words, Christians ought to avoid living like practical atheists in their callings because it is incompatible with what they believe to be true.

In the tense moments that occur in our vocations, we are tempted to forget God is with us. We can believe that our identity is on the line. Even though there is nothing to prove or defend about our worth or acceptance anymore, we forget who we are in Christ and take matters into our own hands. This is called *autonomy*, or living as if God doesn't exist to care for our calling and us. We resort back to autonomous and foolish strategies to make life work apart from God, and joy goes right out the window. Every time we attempt to prove our self-worth, we are like a young man trying to look our absolute best for a girl we want to adore us. We floss for the first time in years, but our happiness is dependent upon others' approval. Christ calls us, however, to declare independence from our jobs, our wealth, and the pressure to attempt our old foolish strategies that do not work.[27]

---

[26] C. S. Lewis, "The Inner Ring," in *The Weight of Glory and Other Addresses* (New York, NY: Simon and Schuster, 1975, repr. 1980), pp. 117-118.

[27] See Robert Davis Smart, *Identity in Christ: Renouncing the Lies and Foolish Strategies* (Bloomington, IN: Westbow Press, 2017).

Autonomous and foolish strategies are in place when we act like orphans, even though our true identity in Christ is as dearly loved children chosen in love out of the orphanage of this fallen world. The story is told of a man going to his family reunion only to meet a woman there who was not part of his family, but rather a guest of one of his female relatives. This man is struck by the woman and wants to meet her. Being unacquainted with how to begin such a relationship, he walks up and uses a wooden and silly opening line saying, "Could you tell me what kind of men you like?" She is taken aback by his directness but replies, "I love American-Indian men. They are really mysterious. I love their lineage, their appreciation of nature. They are majestic and have a strong sense of history. But," she continues, "as I think about it, I also deeply appreciate those of the Jewish heritage. They have left an enormous legacy of endurance under trial, tradition and courage. And you know, being from the South, I like the southern redneck. He's so basic, and not complex. So gutsy and direct." And then she says, "By the way, what's your name?" Thinking quickly on his feet, he replies, "Tonto Rosenberg, but my friends call me Bubba Joe." Our foolish strategies make us we live like practical atheists, even though we are gospel believers. When the impulse hits you under pressure to take matters into your own hands, give pause to that autonomous compulsion and refuse your foolish strategies to make up for what you demanded God to do.

All work and no rest

The fourth hindrance is our failure to rest from our labors and work. Until we learn to deeply rest and separate ourselves from our work, we won't work effectively. Rather, we will be pained with a freneticism that keeps us from enjoying God's call on our lives. We need a rhythm of work and rest in our callings. Our callings include a call to both work and rest—it means that our calling is lived out "in the constant cycle of work and rest."[28]

There is a symbiotic relationship between our calling to Christ (performance) and our identity in Christ (being); between labor and replenishment; between day and night; between weekdays and Sunday. We lose perspective on our calling until we pull away from it. Emotional, intellectual, and physical replenishment leads to a more effective effort in our callings. Wisdom tells us it is better to stop swinging an ax in order to sharpen the blade, even though you swing less often (Ecclesiastes 10:10). Henri Nouwen wrote:

> Aren't you, like me, hoping that some person, thing, or event will come along to give you that final feeling of inner well-being you desire? Don't you often hope: 'May this book, idea, course, trip, job, country or relationship fulfill my deepest desire.' But as long as you are waiting for that mysterious moment you will go on running helter-skelter, always anxious and restless, always lustful and angry, never fully satisfied. You know that this is the compulsiveness that keeps us going and busy, but at the same time makes us wonder whether we are getting anywhere in the long run. This is the way to spiritual exhaustion and burn-out. This is the way to spiritual death.[29]

Exodus 20:9 commands the seventh day to be a day of rest from our principal labors because God rested from His labors on the seventh day after the work of creation. Since rest is tied to creation,

---

[28] Ben Wirtherington, *Work: The Meaning of Your Life* (Grand Rapids, MI: Eerdmans, 2011), p. 2.
[29] Henri J. M. Nouwen, *Life of the Beloved: Spiritual Living in a Secular World* (New York, NY: Crossroad Publishing Company, 2002), p. 35.

overwork violates God's order, causing His creatures to burn out. Taking time for rest requires you to trust God to keep and preserve your job, which He does anyway. He causes the growth for the day of casting seeds and watering. God produces fruit even when you are away. He keeps the world going without you. He is God, who works day and night, and you are not. Josef Pieper asks his audience about their rest from their works: "Do you have a celebratory, approving, lingering gaze of the inner eye upon God's work through your good works to which He called you?"[30]

Jesus promises to give us rest for our souls when we are weary and heavy with burdens. "Come to Me, all who labor and are weary and heavy laden, and I will give you rest. Take My yoke upon you, and learn from Me, for I am gentle and lowly in heart, and you will find rest for your souls" (Matthew 11:28–29). There is a rest Jesus offers, even when we still work under His yoke.

Romanticism

The fifth hindrance is what my friend calls "romanticism"— living an illusion that there is something more than the ordinary. It makes us chase from one great job to another, while unable to find God in the ordinary (Ecclesiastes 2:24, 3:12–13). It is a rejection of the ordinary.[31] Where we are, and the people we are with, are never enough. My friend Zack Eswine helps us appreciate the ordinary because Jesus does. Jesus is more than willing to remove this sort of "romanticism" from ruining our sense of calling:

---

[30] Josef Piper, *Leisure: The Basis of Culture* (San Francisco, CA: Ignatius Press, 2009), p. 33.

[31] See my review of Michael Horton's *Ordinary: Sustainable Faith in a Radical, Restless World* (Grand Rapids, MI: Zondervan, 2014. 224 pp. http://themelios.thegospelcoalition.org/review/ordinary-sustainable-faith-in-a-radical-restless-world-michael-horton

> Therefore, those of you searching for something larger, faster, and more significant, who feel that if you could just be somewhere else doing something else as somebody else, then your life would really matter—Jesus has come to confound you.[32]

Another way to say this is that Jesus didn't rescue us from living out our particular callings in the everyday places where He assigned us. So, when we ask the question about where our place is, we are not asking to leave the ordinary. Rather we are asking where an "ordinary" place is that we might fulfill our extraordinary calling to Christ. The Christian life never removes us from the ordinary places in the world, but it does take us deeper into them.

Consider what every epic battle ends with. Is it not to return things back to the ordinary? Maximus, the protagonist in *The Gladiator* film, returns to his farm. The hobbits return to the shire in Tolkien's *Lord of the Rings* trilogy. What if there is no battle like we imagine, but only loving neighbors well in one place for a long life. What's wrong with a thousand small acts of kindness and hundreds of repeated greetings in one community with rippling effects for generations? The Bible begins and ends with the earth, although it is a new earth when the tree of life shows up again. In Genesis 2, Adam and Eve receive a calling from God to a garden before anything else.

Romanticism hinders our privilege to embody being human in very ordinary places. It would be a miserable life if you were "Mr. Incredible," stuck in an office with a boss that calls you into his office to tell you: "I'm not happy, Bob, not happy." The truth is, however, that you are "Mr. Imperfect." You are finite with weaknesses and

---

[32] Zack Eswine, *Sensing Jesus: Life and Ministry as a Human Being* (Wheaton, IL: Crossway, 2013), p. 40). Eswine explains how "[w]e restlessly move ourselves from one grand moment to the next... We have trouble seeing how it is glorifying to God to eat food, learn to love, go to bed, and get up the next day for work." *Ibid.*, p. 49.

limitations so that Christ's infinite power and incredible grace might be displayed in you.

To respond well to Christ's calling is to embrace your limits. The limits of your place, your family, and your calling to Christ (Hebrews 1:1–3, 2:1–4) are designed for your greatest impact beyond the limits of your imagination. The romantic, however, insists that he is meant to live for "more out there; somewhere." Let's remove such hindrances as idolatry, unhealthy competition, autonomous living, frenetic busyness without rest, and romanticism.

Resignation

The sixth major hindrance to our joy in our calling to Christ is the evil spirit of resignation—becoming resigned to something less than your calling to Christ. This is a big one, at least it was for me. It is an attitude of surrender to worldliness, and it is expressed by hopelessness and quitting.

I was investing time in Dustin, a faithful man, through life-on-life missional discipleship. Since he ran marathons, I suggested we train together for one in Indianapolis. As we trained for months and miles of running, he said that I had a possibility of qualifying for the Boston Marathon. I was seventeen years older and the qualifying time for a forty-eight year old was three-and-a-half hours.

The day of the race came, and our families were there to cheer us on. We made great time and felt all right until mile eighteen, when the mixture of mocha-flavored protein goo and lemon sports drinks did not sit well in my tummy. I said, "I quit." Dustin objected, "You can't quit! Your family will be disappointed." The first time I saw them during the race they were eating Culver's butter burgers and drinking concrete milkshakes. They were having fun together, but I thought to myself, "I better finish." Somehow I got my legs moving until I hit another wall.

At mile twenty-four I said to Dustin, "I quit." He said, "Don't quit!" Just then a man ten years older than me passed us and said, "You guys trying to make 3:30? You can do it." He ran with a limp and passed us up. I said, "Fine!" I imitated his limping style and made it to mile twenty-five with only one mile to go. That is when I said for a third time to Dustin, "I quit." There was a hill in front of us that seemed like the steepest mountain I had ever seen. The mocha protein goo and sports drinks were swirling around in my tummy. Dustin took off up the hill without me. With that, I raced up to him. Dustin said, "Slow down. We have to make it all the way to the finish."

When we came to the finish line, there was my family chomping on Culver's butter burgers and drinking concrete milkshakes to cheer me on. I crossed the finish line just after Dustin at 3:17:03. Do you know what was so wonderful about that? It wasn't that I had the privilege to run another marathon in six months in Boston. It was that I could quit.

When we get to heaven, one of the most wonderful things we can do is rest. Only then, we can quit. We can sit or walk; we can lie down or shout for joy, but we can finally quit the race. Eugene Peterson wrote:

> The essential thing 'in heaven and earth' is ... that there should be long obedience in the same direction; there thereby results, and has always resulted in the long run, something which has made life worth living.[33]

The curse on masculinity is made to make every male admit he's licked so he will cry out for grace and salvation from Christ, instead

---

[33] Eugene Peterson, *A Long Obedience in the Same Direction* (Downers Grove, IL: InterVarsity Press, 1980), p. 247.

of simply giving up and returning to the dirt too early. Resignation is a spirit of death; it tempts us to quit the race. We hear it in prayers of resignation that trust God for nothing in a tone of defeat. We speak messages of resignation when we tell people, "Don't work too hard." We believe the curse has the final word when cynicism rules us while we work and consider the future. We live lifestyles of resignation when we plan for nothing more than an empty retirement that has no intentionality for the kingdom of God and eternal rewards. Albert Camus wrote about "The Myth of Syphisus." The gods caught Syphisus giving celestial secrets to mortals, which had been going on for a long time. His punishment was to roll a huge rock up a huge hill all day long, every day. It would be like being chained to a CPU data entry activity all day, and ten minutes before every day ended, the computer crashes. The next day is a repeat of the last day. Hell is the experience of executing for all eternity an endless act from which nothing ever matters.

The curse on feminity is made to make every female admit that her desire is too much for intimacy, to know and be known, so that she will admit she's licked and cry out for another man; namely Jesus Christ. He shall crush and slay the dragon. He has crushed the serpent's head on the cross, will cast all demons into hell, and will marry bride. He will protect her from dialoging with the evil one and not stand by her in silence and passivity like the first Adam (Genesis 3:6; Isaiah 62:1–7). Instead of closing the womb of her heart to relationships, she can embrace the sorrow that only Christ can satisfy her deepest desire that tempts her to remain a controlling woman.

Christ has freed us from being resigned to merely live without hope, purpose, and a calling to Christ that counts for eternity in the routines of life in a fallen world. As Fyodor Dostoevsky put it:

For the secret of man's being is not only to live ...
but to live for something definite. Without a firm
notion of what he is living for, man will not accept
life and will rather destroy himself the remain on
earth.[34]

The "Should" Gun

Let us consider the last two major hindrances to joy in our calling to Christ. The seventh major hindrance is rooted in our self-righteousness and bitterness when we keep the "should" gun pointed at our heads. The "should" gun is a substitute for the gospel, which we *should* keep pointed at our heads. Whereas when the gospel is ruling us, we work out of an assurance that we are pardoned of all our sins and accepted as righteous in God's sight (we are justified), this other voice, however, is a killjoy because it adds "shoulds" to our consciences that God never required of us. It could be the "shoulds" of the world about where you work, or the ones of a parent about what you *should* do as a vocation. It makes our callings impossible to fulfill because we struggle with failure more than is necessary. It is related to perfectionism, and cuts the roots of grace within.

Have you ever felt this? Have you been living out of the heart God gave you, or trying to come through in a calling that someone else put on your shoulders? Many people feel stuck without adventure because they have a job their parents told them they ought to do. They live with a snarly self-righteous anger that others are experiencing more joy in their callings, and see themselves as the self-righteous older brother waiting for his father to recognize all his dutiful labors.

Maybe the should-gun is not only pointed at you, but also at

---

[34] Fyodor Dostoevsky, *The Brothers Karamazov* (The Inquisitor) is quoted in Os Guiness, *The Call: Finding and Fulfilling the Central Purpose of Your Life* (Nashville, TN: Word Publishing, 1998), p. 2.

others—even your Father in heaven. Put it down for Christ's sake, and discover His call on your life, which God intended for you to live out with the desires and joy He made you for.

The "should" gun tells us that we are to do too many things that God never called us to do. We must embrace our limitations and not over-extend ourselves too far. John Calvin counsels Christians to live within the limitations God has placed upon our finite lives. Calvin wrote that believers must

> learn to measure carefully their powers, lest they should wear out, by ambitiously embracing too many occupations. For the propensity to engage in too many things ... is a very common malady ... God has so arranged our condition, that individuals are only endued with a certain measure of gifts ... The Lord bids each one of us in all life's actions to look to his calling. For He knows what great restlessness human nature flames, with what fickleness it is borne hither and thither, how its ambition longs to embrace various things at once. Therefore, lest through our stupidity and rashness everything be turned topsy-turvy, He has appointed duties for every man and woman in his particular way of life. And that no one may thoughtlessly transgress his limits, He has named various kinds of living "callings." Therefore each individual has his own kind of living assigned to him by the Lord as a sort of sentry post so that he may not heedlessly wander about through life.[35]

---

[35] John Calvin, *Institutes of the Christian Religion* (Philadelphia, PA: The Westminster Press, 1960), 3.10.6, Volume One, p. 724.

Fear and Anxiety

Finally, there is the hindrance of fear. If you are ruled by a fear, then that fear is your god. Catastrophists subscribe to a catastrophic theory of what is to come. They anticipate a dreadful future, rather than a good one. This isn't just a matter of age, for even youth are beginning to fear the commitment required to enter into particular callings that Christ summons them into—whether it is joining a local church, pursuing employment, or risking a proposal when they want to marry. It is commonly understood in our time that young people are delaying or putting off such callings.

What is happening in our culture with regard to delaying adulthood—putting off other options, vocational, and relational commitments? Sociologists researched a new phenomenon among young adults who prolong adolescence into their twenties and thirties. Parents are increasingly willing to extend support, financial and otherwise, to their children between eighteen and thirty years of age.[36] Of the many factors studied, fear of commitment and the future prospect of particular callings is a major hindrance.

Fear is also related to anxiety, and anxiety is not only an internal experience of individuals. Anxiety exists in systems—families, churches, and workplaces. The late Edwin Friedman has offered a helpful leadership theory, which is easy to understand and apply in overcoming anxiety in the places and systems God called us to serve.

Staying Warmly Present

Friedman argues that effective leadership is not about possessing certain traits, techniques, skills, or maybe even by being tall.

---

[36] See Christian Smith with Patricia Snell, *Souls in Transition: The Religious & Spiritual Lives of Emerging Adults* (New York: Oxford University Press, 2008), p. 6.

In *A Failure of Nerve*, Friedman goes against the grain of other theories of leadership.[37] Rather, he argues that it is an emotional process of regulating one's own anxiety. This process is called self-differentiation, a theory rooted in cell biology. Healthy cells have a nucleus, which governs the activities they were designed for, and a strong wall or membrane, which keeps them separate from others and protects their nucleus when they are around other cells.

A differentiated person is like a healthy cell that can stay connected to others without losing his or her identity and without taking on the anxiety of the group. A differentiated leader can take a well-defined stand even when others in the group disagree, while still remaining connected in a meaningful way.

The problem with anxiety in a family, church, or workplace is that there are poorly differentiated people who act like viruses. Viruses do not possess a healthy identity in Christ. They lack a sense of calling to Christ, or a core identifying principle, which makes it impossible for them to exist on their own. Rather, they look for other poorly differentiated others, equally at risk, who are easy to latch on to. Is this harmless workplace chatter or gossip? The problem is they are infecting the system with their own anxiety. They can't handle one-on-one conflict with another, so they triangle in less differentiated others and form an unhealthy emotion bond of anxiety. Such enmeshment will increase anxiety in the place, causing stress and burnout over other people's problems.

One leader who can offer his or her non-anxious presence will help others solve their own problems responsibly. The key to overcoming anxiety in one's calling is to, in my terms, "stay warmly present." Staying warmly present by tolerating others' anxieties will help them to own their responsibilities without infecting others.

---

[37] Edwin H. Friedman, *A Failure of Nerve: Leadership in the Age of the Quick Fix* (Seabury Books, 2007).

Staying warmly present in a differentiated manner diffuses the anxiety in the places God put us.

Anxiety Sabotage within the Community

Some organizations, like churches or work environments, are chronically anxious. In other words, the majority of the people in the place are poorly differentiated like cells without nuclei or membrane walls. They are not secure in their identities or clear about their callings. You will threaten such a system if you are warmly present to them. You will upset the way things have always been—the homeostasis of the organization. This in turn will inevitably lead to the formation of a coup against the differentiated leader.

Sabotage against a differentiated leader is exactly the sign indicating that you are healthy and warmly present for their welfare. If you remain warmly present in any place long enough, the anxiety in the system will eventually diminish to all-time lows. People will enjoy their particular callings because you stayed warmly present on their behalf.

Practice the Spiritual Discipline of Solitude

One of the best disciplines for Christians to renounce the hindrances of idolatry, unhealthy competition, autonomy living, frenetic busyness without rest, romanticism, resignation, pointing of the "should-gun," and anxious fear is to get in front of God's face and voice in silence. There you can hear His voice and examine yourself to see if any of these obstacles are hindering you in your calling to Christ.

Ask Christ which of these hindrances is most clearly keeping you from a joyful response to His calling for your life. Write out prayers of renunciation for each hindrance with an earnest desire to come alive to His summons to live life abundantly. You may want to read 2 Corinthians 7:11 and John 10:10.

Henri Nouwen describes how such a practice may not only be difficult for us, but also extremely beneficial. He describes it this way:

> As soon as we are alone ... inner chaos opens up in us. This chaos can be so disturbing and so confusing that we can hardly wait to get busy again. Entering a private room and shutting the door, therefore, does not mean that we immediately shut out all our inner doubts, anxieties, fears, bad memories, unresolved conflicts, angry feelings and impulsive desires. On the contrary, when we have removed our outer distraction, we often find that our inner distraction manifest themselves to us in full force. We often use the outer distractions to shield ourselves from the interior noises. This makes the discipline of solitude all the more important.[38]

Group Discussion Questions:

1. Am I happy to be in God's presence now without any other gods pushing or pulling me from His smile over me (Zephaniah 3:17)?
2. Name the idols that demand sacrifices to their altars that promise you satisfied longings. Have you been sacrificing loved ones, money, energy, and others' reputations to an idol?

---

[38] Henri Nouwen, *Making All Things New and Other Classics* (New York, NY: Ballentine Books, 1983), pp. 69-71.

3. Would you be willing to confess to Christ how your approach to His calling on your life has often been mixed with your autonomous strategies to obtain satisfaction without soaking up His grace, without taking time to learn wisdom from Him, without exercising the Spirit's gifting and power, and often despising the place where He put you to fulfill good works He predestined for you to do?
4. Do you rest from works? Do you enjoy your works? Do you take time to reflect how to improve effectiveness? Do you involve God in a strategic planning process for home, your principal work, and peripheral works? Is there rest beneath your rest? Are you sleeping well? Are you treating your body with as much love as Jesus has for it?
5. Are you truly glad for 1 Thessalonians 4:11–12? Are you surrendered to the place God set you in? Are you growing in intimacy with your primary relationships?
6. Have you resigned to something less than your Christian longings cry out for? Are you afraid to live with unmet longings no matter the level of sorrow in order to trust God with them, rather than live like a robotic, mechanic zombie in your calling?
7. Have you put the "should" gun down and started living moment by moment from the new heart God gave you? Do you live out of your true identity in Christ or under condemnation, hoping to overcome Satan's lie concerning you?

Chapter 4
Sensing God's Call on your Life

How to Sense God's Call

In order to capture a clearer sense of your calling we will do four things together. First, we hope to discover the longings God has given us. Second, we will ask God to help us interpret God's providence in our lives through the Holy Spirit. Third, we will apply Micah 6:8 by asking ourselves three questions based on three virtues God requires in our callings. Fourth, we will consider what burden or message God is putting on your heart to deliver to significant others in your life.

Discover Your Longings

When God took out our heart of stone, He put in a heart of flesh. He calls us to live out of the tender heart He gave us, which includes our longings. What do you long for? Longings and desires for knowing Christ, winning the lost, and loving people well are the fuel God gave us to move forward with tenderness in our callings.

Counselor Larry Crabb helpfully describes three types of

longings.[39] These three types of longings are designated as our casual, critical, and crucial longings. First, there are casual longings for better circumstances and new provisions. Your casual longings may be for a clean house by the end of the day, a pay increase by year's end, or a good dinner tonight. Second, there are critical longings for deeper relationships and God's blessings for others. You may long for reconciliation with a family member, for a closer relationship to your spouse, or for a child to be saved. Third, there are crucial longings for God's unconditional love and for Himself. It is a longing to be satisfied in God and to walk closely with Him.

These three types of longings must be embraced and not dismissed. To embrace them is to embrace the sorrow of unmet longings. Perhaps this was the reason why Jesus was called "a man of sorrows" (Isaiah 53; Hebrews 5:7). Your longings tell you that you have glory; that you were built for God and a better day. The reason why nothing will ultimately satisfy us in this life is because we were made for glory and the new earth. Creation, the Holy Spirit within us, and ourselves all groan together until we experience the fullness and satisfaction in God that we were created for (Romans 8:18–30).

In *The Silver Chair,* C. S. Lewis portrays how Christ, represented by Aslan the Lion, knows that we, like Jill, have these deep thirsts and longings. When we are thirsty, however, we have learned to deaden these longings because longings are dangerous and have been an occasion of pain and risk. Lewis wrote:

> "Are you not thirsty?" said the Lion. "I am dying of thirst," said Jill. "Then drink," said the Lion. "May I—could I—would you mind going away while I do?" said Jill. The Lion answered this only by a look and a very low growl. And as Jill gazed at its motionless bulk, she realized that she might as well

---

[39] Larry Crabb, *InsideOut* (Colorado Springs, CO: NavPress, 1988), pp. 80-81.

have asked the whole mountain to move aside for her convenience. The delicious rippling noise of the stream was driving her nearly frantic. "Will you promise not to—do anything to me, if I do come?" said Jill. "I make no promise," said the Lion. Jill was so thirsty now that, without noticing it, she had come a step nearer. "Do you eat girls?" she said. "I have swallowed up girls and boys, women and men, kings and emperors, cities and realms," said the Lion. It didn't say this as if it were boasting, nor as if it were sorry, nor as if it were angry. It just said it. "I daren't come and drink," said Jill. "Then you will die of thirst," said the Lion. "Oh dear!" said Jill, coming another step nearer. "I suppose I must go and look for another stream then." "There is no other stream," said the Lion."[40]

In Narnia there is only one fountain to satisfy our longings; namely, in Christ. Therefore, we would never want to deaden these longings. Rather, these longings are meant to make us lean into the future with hope. They fuel our callings. They cause our deepest emotions to surface, which is one reason why people are afraid of them. So often we are embarrassed to cry in front of others when we express them, but this is an illegitimate shame because these tearful longings express our groans for our future glory. People in touch with their longings have a heart that is present to Christ, people, and place.

Interpreting Two Events in Your Life

Scripture uses two words for time; namely, chronological time

---

[40] C. S. Lewis, *The Silver Chair* (New York: NY: HarperTrophy, 1981), pp. 19-21.

on your cell phone or calendar and a significant moment or season when God is at work. The former is the word *chronos* and the latter is the word *kairos*.[41]

By identifying two "kairotic" events in your life, we may ask God for how them to shape you for your general and particular callings. First, take time to select one kairotic event or moment in your life when you were transformed by love and grace. It doesn't have to be your conversion. It may be when someone showed you that God has a great purpose and future for your life. It is a moment when you felt life is precious and your life is deeply connected to others. Second, remember another kairotic moment or event when you were deeply wounded or were placed in the furnace of affliction. It is a moment when you were painfully aware that you needed God to redeem a situation or your family.

God ordained these two kairotic events or moments in order to shape you for sensing His calling for your life. The first event may have been a discovery of where your greatness in life lies, and the other may be the occasion in the present where your compassion is felt. God uses everything for good, even our worst moments (Romans 8:28). Joseph's worst painful event was experienced when his brothers were cruel to him. At the end of his life he told his brothers, "You meant it for evil, but God meant it for good" (Genesis 50:20). Joseph interpreted God's providence—His sustaining and ruling all things toward His good purpose—as the key to understanding his calling.

These two kairotic moments, then, are the matter you can use to sense God's calling on your life to live for Christ's glory. Robert Bly seemed to capture this when he wrote:

---

[41] The word *kairos* was an ancient Greek word meaning "opportunity," "season," or "fitting time." Another Greek word for "time" was *chronos*. A sequence of moments was expressed as *chronos*, emphasizing the duration of the time; an appointed time was expressed as *kairos*, with no regard for the length of the time. Thus, *chronos* was more linear and quantitative, and *kairos* was more nonlinear and qualitative.

> Where a man's wound is, that is where his genius will be. Wherever the wound appears in our soul, that is exactly where we will give our major gift to the community.[42]

We can listen and read how God authored our story and our faith and see where He places us. Kairos is story time. It provides the clues that are impregnated with meaning about how God is calling us to act in the present. These kairotic events are like the statue of the Kairos god standing outside the Olympic Stadium of Greece, which called the athletes to seize the moment. God puts within each of us individual gifts, talents, and strengths, which help us to "hear" His voice and to fulfill our calling. It is kind of like discovering our own unique fingerprint, retina, voiceprint, and DNA, if we are courageous enough to identify these two kairotic events. David Brooks wrote:

> These circumstances give us the great chance to justify our gifts. Your ability to discern your vocation depends on the condition of your eyes and ears, whether they are sensitive enough to understand the assignment your context is giving you.[43]

God ordained our earthly father as the primary one to name us and separate us from our mother in adolescence. God ordained him as the primary voice to call us out of ourselves and up to our heavenly Father to receive His voice; to hear, "You are my beloved son/daughter in whom I am well pleased." Then we are to receive our

---

[42] Robert Bly, *Iron John: A Book About Men* (New York: Vintage Books, 1990), p. 42.

[43] David Brooks, *The Road to Character* (New York, NY: Random House, 2015), p. 24.

father's empowerment and be sent out and into the world in response to God's voice and calling.

Calling is a beautiful aspect of gospel formation. Your calling from God to Christ is never at stake. It doesn't depend on a job interview or any fearful loss of a position in a particular calling. We may rest. If you try to keep it, then you will lose it. Lose your call for Jesus sake, and you will keep it. It is always there, even after periods of dormancy or dullness of hearing. It remains with us as we seek to hear God's voice in scripture. Peter failed, but his call remained the same. Christ came to remind him of his calling after Peter's threefold failure and denial of Christ. Jesus isn't looking for a replacement for you. Your calling to Christ is as unique as your thumbprint.

Since calling is the key to tracing the story line of our lives and interpreting the meaning of our existence in a chaotic, noisy, and fatherless world, we praise God that His grace is unchanging. He intends to make us glad in Him so that He may be glorified in us. When Peter Marshall grew up in Scotland in a Christian home, he refused his mother's good intentions for his health. She insisted that he eat his prunes, and Peter refused. A struggle of wills ensued. "Peter," his mother said. "Now God won't like this. God doesn't like little boys to refuse to finish all their prunes." Peter went up to his room, and he closed his bedroom door behind him. There he sat and sulked over the prunes. It wasn't but a few minutes when a terrible thunderstorm came. His mother went up to see how little Peter was doing, and there he was at the window looking at the sheets of rain, listening to the thunder, and saying, "My, my, sic a fuss to mak' ower twa prunes."[44]

One of my great joys in my calling has been to invest my life as a spiritual father into fatherless young men who face and name their father-wounds in a way that helps them see the fatherlessness

---

[44] Catherine Marshall, *A Man Called Peter: The Story of Peter Marshall* (Grand Rapids, MI: Baker, 1951), p. 176.

in men they can disciple. In the words of Frederick Buechner: "The place where God calls you is the place where your deep gladness and the world's deep hunger meet."[45]

Bryan and I meet every week for discipleship. We met right after he got out of prison. He grew up in the projects of Chicago, and Satan told him he would never amount to anything of worth. A second grade teacher told him in his classroom that he would never rise above the poverty level and lifestyle of those in the projects of Chicago. The two kairotic events in his story were the day his father took him to make and fly a kite, and the day when he became fatherless. His life fell apart when his father died of alcoholism. Bryan made a judgment on God— that all God does is "take." He hardened his heart to spiritual fathers, pastors in particular, and became a drug dealer as a gang member until he was incarcerated for a number of years. Finally, he was released, and we met for the first time.

Bryan was converted to Christ and began coming to our church. He is my spiritual son, you might say, and I am his spiritual father. He renounced the lie that he will never rise above the lifestyle of poverty and project culture. He has a good job, a home, and makes a decent living. What excites Bryan, however, is not only meeting one on one together in my office in discipleship, but also Bryan loves spending all his free time reaching out to the boys in the projects in our city. He is a father in a certain sense with a couple handfuls of young boys singing Christian rap and attending church on Sundays for worship. God uses the two kairotic events in our lives for good to shape us in the spiritual formation season of calling.

Well, then, what shall we say about the painful and kairotic events in our past? Let us name what happened, taking every thought captive that is raised up against the knowledge of God (2

---

[45] Frederick Buechner, *Wishful Thinking: A Seeker's ABC* (New York, NY: HarperCollins, 1973), pp. 118-119.

Corinthians 10:4–5). God will redeem it for good and make you particularly useful in the lives of others with similar wounds. Henri Nouwen writes about the healing this process truly is:

> The man who [can] articulate the movements of his inner life, who can give names to his varied experiences, need no longer be a victim of himself, but is able to slowly and consistently to remove the obstacles that prevent the spirit from entering. He is able to create space for Him whose heart is greater than his, whose eyes see more than his, and whose hands can heal more than his.[46]

Three Questions of Micah 6:8

> He has showed you, O man, what is good. And what does the LORD require of you? To act justly and to love mercy and to walk humbly with your God. (Micah 6:8)

This verse of scripture highlights three virtues that shall furnish us for sensing our callings to Christ. We will ask it three questions in a personal way in order to discover how it applies to you individually. The three virtues are justice, mercy, and humility. The three questions from these three virtues only you can answer.

What makes you angry?

The first is justice. Act justly. Justice makes a Christian ask herself what makes me angry? There are injustices in our contemporary

---

[46] Henri Nouwen, *The Wounded Healer: Ministry in Contemporary Society* (New York, NY: Doubleday, 1972), p. 38.

culture and oppression exists in our world that arouse a holy anger (Ephesians 4:26) in our hearts. Which one(s) make you slam your fist down and say, "No more?" Is it poverty? Is it economic injustice? Is it Internet theft? What makes you angry for justice? This righteous anger can energize you to take action in the particular calling God is summoning you into.

One of the men I have investing my life into, I also led to Christ. He is married, and they have just adopted a boy from a far-away nation. I'll name him "Thankful Beloved." If you asked this couple what makes them angry in a godly sense, you will see tears come down from their eyes as they tell you it is that there exist in this world too many unwanted children. They have a sense of calling to adopt the unwanted, and they have a very large family now. This is what makes them long for justice. This is what makes them angry. This is what brings them to surrender to the Father, who chose them in love out of the orphanage of a fallen world to be His beloved. The woman wrote me recently about her newly adopted son's unwillingness to surrender to his dad's will. She wrote something like this: "As I held this little boy in my arms and begged God to help my adopted son surrender, I also, in a sense, surrendered my own adopted heart to my heavenly Father."

What makes you weep?

The second is mercy. "Love mercy." God's mercy is better than life. Jesus would often tell the self-righteous to go and ponder that God loves mercy more than our sacrifices. Mercy makes a Christian ask herself what makes me weep? Hannah wept for the privilege to have a child (1 Samuel 1:10). As soon as Nehemiah heard the words about the brokenness in God's people he wept (Nehemiah 1:4). Esther fell at her feet and wept for the evil Haman plotted to kill God's people, kind of like the unborn aborted today (Esther

8:3). Jesus said, "Blessed are those who mourn" like Him (Matthew 5:4; 23:37; John 11:35; Psalm 137). What makes you weep with compassion? Is it the unborn? Is it for the salvation of people? God gave you this holy sorrow for others.

When the famous missionary to China, William C. Burns, was raised in a Christian home in Kilsyth, Scotland, his mother took him shopping in the big city of Glasgow. During the shopping trip William's mother lost his son in the crowds. When she finally found her son, who was a young teenager, she discovered him with tears streaming down his face. "Willie, my son, what ails you?" she asked with deep concern. William was struck by the sound of so many footsteps pounding on the pavement and wooden floors. William replied to his mother, "Oh, Mother! Mother! The thud of these Christless feet on their way to hell breaks my heart."

This was a kairotic moment for William that shaped his sense of calling. William grew up, dressed and cut his hair like a Chinese teacher. He joined Hudson Taylor, each on a boat along a river, taking turns preaching to the Chinese along the banks of the river. When he died after a successful ministry of evangelism, a small box came back to his family containing all his belongings—a Bible and a spiritual journal. What makes you weep?

What makes you walk?

The third is humility. "Walk humbly with your God." Humility makes a Christian ask herself, *What do I love to do?* What makes you take steps? The Qoheleth said that there is nothing better than to find enjoyment in one's calling (Ecclesiastes 2:24). The key is to walk to the end; to get started and to finish; to launch out and to depend on God until the end.

In John Steinbeck's *Cannery Row* there is a character named Henri who never takes steps to fulfill his calling. Henri is a local artist and a friend of Doc's. No one is certain about Henri's artistic abilities, but everyone agrees he's doing a beautiful job building his boat. The boat has always been on locks in a vacant lot and has never been in the ocean. It is Henri's unfinished life work, however, because Henri is afraid of the ocean. Steinbeck wrote about a conversation between Hazel and Doc as they spoke about Henri's issues:

> Doc chuckled. "He still building his boat?"
> "Sure," said Hazel. "He's got it all changed around. New kind of a boat. I guess he'll take it apart and change it. Doc—is he nuts?"
> Doc swung his heavy sack of starfish to the ground and stood panting a little. "Nuts?" he asked. "Oh, yes, I guess so. Nuts about the same amount we are, only in a different way."
> Such a thing had never occurred to Hazel. He looked upon himself as a crystal pool of clarity and on his life as a troubled glass of misunderstood virtue. Doc's last statement had outraged him a little. "But that boat—" he cried. "He's been building that boat for seven years that I know of. The blocks rotted out and he made concrete blocks. Every time he gets it nearly finished he changes it and starts over again. I think he's nuts. Seven years on a boat."
>
> Doc was sitting on the ground pulling off his rubber boots. "You don't understand," he said gently. "Henri loves boats but he's afraid of the ocean."
> "What's he want a boat for then?" Hazel demanded.
>
> "He likes boats," said Doc. "But suppose he finishes his boat. Once it's finished people will say, 'Why don't you put it in the water?' Then if he puts it in

the water, he'll have to go out in it, and he hates the water. So you see, he never finishes the boat—so he doesn't ever have to launch it."[47]

We must walk humbly with God in our callings without refusing to finish what we began, and without fearing the completion.

What arouses your anger when you see evil score another victory? Where does your heart break with sorrow from what is still unredeemed? What brings a "yes" to your soul when you start walking with God in order to give yourself away?

A New Zealand pastor used the workbook material I had developed for the four seasons of spiritual formation. He informed me that his spiritual formation group on calling has had a deep impact on many people. One such person is a British immigrant named Susan. Susan became a Christian at university in South Africa. After she was married with children, she and her family immigrated to New Zealand. Her family has struggled finding their place in New Zealand, constantly wondering if they made the best decision immigrating. Part of their problem was that for years they didn't connect to a church home, which led to a weakening of their faith and family. Susan and her husband did not join a small group designed for spiritual growth until this six-week series on calling to Christ. The pastor mentioned that during the last session, when the entire group was taking turns reading their sense of personal calling, Susan said, "For the first time I have freedom knowing my place, and I have lost the guilt of feeling that I am a disappointment to God just being a mother. I have always had a sense that what I do as a mother is not as important as what others do for Jesus in the church or workplace. I am free from that now to get on with the great and high calling of motherhood, and to rest in the place God

---

[47] John Steinbeck, *Cannery Row* (New York, NY: Penguin Books, 1945, repr. 1992), chapter six, (Kindle Locations 440-455).

has us." God has used the spiritual formation studies on identity and calling to restore this family in their marriage, parenting, and love for Christ.

Deliver the Mail

When we own our longings, trust God with them in our calling to Christ, and answer the three questions from Micah, we may feel the burden to be delivered to another (others) who are placed strategically in our path. We must deliver the message from the depth of our being; we must "deliver the mail" that has not yet been delivered, and therefore not read.

Recently we enjoyed a visit from Dave and Cathy Bowman. They are fruitful Navigator staff for the college campuses, and invested their lives into us from the time we were twenty. After we had our final meal together, I thought about the usual goodbyes we would exchange. God, however, put a burden on my heart to say how much I appreciate them for their callings and for loving us so well. Self-protection hindered me within because I knew I would cry in front of them, as my longings and this oracle would come forth. I had to deliver the mail. As we stood in a parking lot, I took hold of each of their shoulders one at a time to say how much I loved them and thanked God for each of them. I delivered the mail while looking them in the eyes, face to face. You may have guessed that I cried as I shared the message. An oracle for a prophet was literally a burden. Dan Allender explains:

> God has crafted each of us with burdens we can't escape. A burden is something that breaks our heart, tightens our fists, and compels us to cry out yes! When redemption comes ... [a] burden may be concrete (AIDS), theoretical (rightly dividing the

Word), cultural (racism, sexism, ageism, abuse), situational (Irish missions), or relational (caring for an aging parent) ... [a] burden is a passion that typically arises from the mesh of our story.[48]

In order to capture a clearer sense of our calling, we covered four areas together, but now you must put them to practice. First, take time to discover the casual, critical, and crucial longings God has given you. Second, ask God to help you interpret His providence in your life through the Holy Spirit by seeing how the two kairotic events are shaping your sense of calling. Third, apply Micah 6:8 to your sense of calling by asking yourselves three questions based on the three virtues God requires in our callings. Fourth, consider what burden or message God is putting on your heart to deliver to significant others in your life.

My dear friend, Zack Eswine, sent me an email recently that included a short poem by William Stafford, along with Zack's commentary on it. It teaches me that our stories, our kairotic moments, our longings and burdens, and hearts all make up a "thread to follow" the Lord's callings, while letting go of "threads not given." Here is his email:

> The Way It Is
> There's a thread that you follow. It goes among things that change. But it doesn't change ...
>
> While you hold it you can't get lost. Tragedies happen; people get hurt or die;and you suffer and get old. Nothing you do can stop time's unfolding. You don't ever let go of the thread.

---

[48] Dan Allender, *The Healing Path: How The Hurts In Your Past Can Lead You To A More Abundant Life* (Colorado Springs, CO: WaterBrook Press, 1999), pp. 206–207.

> I find this helpful. Remembering our active attentiveness to discerning, accepting and owning the thread of God's calling and grace in our lives and gradually in his love letting go of threads not given. I love you,
> Zachary[49]

In the final scene from the movie *Amazing Grace,* the British Parliament convened for the abolition of slavery. All eyes were on William Wilberforce, who had a holy anger against the slave trade. He wept for the slaves and was summoned by God to speak up for their freedom. After many years of contending, one defeat after another, he finally saw the victory he had hoped and suffered for. The scene is moving. This is the speech was given in honor of Wilberforce by Lord Charles Fox:

> When people speak of great men, they think of men like Napoleon—men of violence. Rarely do they think of peaceful men. But contrast the reception they will receive when they return home from their battles. Napoleon will arrive in pomp and in power, a man who's achieved the very summit of earthly ambition. And yet his dreams will be haunted by the oppressions of war. William Wilberforce, however, will return to his family, lay his head on his pillow and remember: the slave trade is no more.[50]

After these words, Wilberforce received a standing ovation from the entire House and the Gallery. Discovering our sense of calling

---

[49] Zack quoted from William Stafford, *The Way It Is: New and Selected Poems* (Minneapolis, MN: Graywolf Press, 1998).

[50] Stephen Knight, *Amazing Grace* (FourBoys Films, released February 23, 2007); http://www.imdb.com/title/tt0454776/quotes

to Christ on behalf of others will lead to such an end. May we have the courage to live out our callings, which is the subject of the next chapter.

Discussion Questions for Groups:

1. Ask the Father in Jesus's Name for the Holy Spirit to bring to mind two kairotic events—tragic and redemptive—that He is using to shape you for His calling on your life. How do you think God is using these to shape your calling to Christ?
2. Can you write out the longings—casual, critical, and crucial—and ask God to satisfy these, while embracing the sorrow that you must live with them unmet for now?
3. Pray over Micah 6:8. How would you answer the questions and spell out the answers. What makes you angry (act justly)? What makes you weep (love mercy)? What makes you happy when doing what God designed you to do (walk humbly with your God)?

Identify the burden of a message (oracle) that you ought to deliver to someone. How does it echo the gospel and bless the listener(s)?

Chapter 5
Living out Your Calling to Christ

Now we are ready to live out our callings, practically speaking. We have defined calling to Christ, and understood the theological foundation for it. Hopefully we have begun to remove any hindrances to joy in our callings. This makes us better able to hear God's call on our life. We have taken time to embrace our longings in light of our particular callings. We have applied the three virtues of Micah 6:8 by asking three questions about the hearts God gave each of us. Some of us have identified a heavy, weighty message that God set within us. This is a message for someone we love, and some of us have "delivered the mail." This chapter instructs us how to live out our callings with a threefold expression, banded to a missional community of believers, and in the place God put us.

A Threefold Expression in Relation to Others

God called the Christian to serve others. Since Jesus came in the New Testament to fulfill His calling, we are in the New Covenant. The three Old Testament offices were the prophet, the priest, and the king. They mediated for God to people an exposure of need, an invitation to enjoy worship, and an offer to equip them for war.

When Jesus came, He fulfilled all three offices in the New Covenant as the one true mediator between God and people (1 Timothy 2:5). He is *the* prophet (Deuteronomy 18:18), the King of kings (Revelation 19:16), and the great high priest (Hebrews 4:14), but He also equipped every Christian to exercise all three in their callings. We are a *royal* (kings) *priesthood* (priests) delivered out of the kingdom of darkness to *proclaim* (prophets) God's excellencies before a watching world (1 Peter 2:9).

When we envision the Christian in a royal way as a king, we are thinking of three primary ways to fulfill one's calling like an Old Testament king. We are called to defend God's people from evil, equip an army for battle against an evil kingdom, and cast a bright vision for others' future. When we express our prophetic role, we capture others in their folly. It is an expression of one who primarily disrupts people in order to catch them in their folly. When we think about our priesthood, we consider how to invite others to be glad in God and worship through the sacrifice of the Lamb of God. We are disruptive, inviting, and visionary leaders all in one.

What does this look like? It starts with having a vision for what others can become, like a king, and being willing to equip them for war against evil. It starts in your war room with vision and prayer. For example, what is your vision for others? If God really got a hold of them, what would they look like in five years or more? Do you have a plan to see them equipped into effective soldiers for Christ? It begins with a vision for others, which is born out of prayer with the King of kings.

Secondly, we must face where the people we are called to love are stuck in their foolish strategies to attempt to make their life work apart from God. Love requires not only a vision for what they can become in Christ, but also courage to make them see how they are behaving without Christ. We must be willing to disrupt and catch people in the act of folly. When we catch them, it is not for the purpose of condemning or leaving them. Rather it is always to invite them to worship Christ through His forgiving acceptance.

Finally, it involves an invitation to experience grace through the forgiveness and love of Christ. There is no way we will ever see gospel transformation without a plain invitation to come into the presence of God for acceptance and pardon of all our sins. Only then will we possess a childlike willingness to obey our loving Father, and slave-motivated fear will transform into a joyful choice.

A father is called to offer a threefold expression to his children. Let's say a father is praying for his son each morning, and God lays a vision on the father's heart for what his son could look like should God get a hold of his son's heart. This father, however, knows his son has been rather lifeless and lacking passion as a teenager. Could it be pornography related? So, however uncomfortable it is, the father plans a prophetic disruption in order to catch his son in his folly.

One late night, while the son is in his room on the computer, the father quietly walks in behind his son. The son is exposed, shame pulsates through him, and his father's face and eyes tell him his loving father has caught him. The father doesn't go into a tirade like most dads, however; he comes warmly present to his son and invites him to worship through Jesus's sacrificial love on the cross. Then, after an experience of gospel transformation his son will always remember, this father tells his son how he had a vision for what the boy could become and a plan to get there. So, the father invites his son (priestly) whom he had caught (prophetic) into a future that would equip the boy to become a godly man (kingly). This approach is practical and comprehensive, and has functioned in my particular callings on a number of occasions and situations.

A Band of Brothers (Sisters) Sent by God[51]

The word *apostle* means "a sent one," or one who is to go forth to deliver the gospel. Since the gospel is a communal project, we are to be a community of "sent ones." Most of our pilgrimage and sojourning in life is not to be traveled alone, but with a few kindred spirits. Ask God to give you a few soul mates, fellow pilgrims who are on a similar journey in their callings. As you band together, each must leave the comforts of "the shire" and their false identities. This tight-knit team must cleave together in order to risk for the cause of Christ. A Christian band of brothers and sisters exists to create momentum in inviting like-minded pilgrims to fight, suffer, and celebrate for a larger purpose than they could have otherwise lived for on their own.

Such a band of saints is in a real sense an *ekklesia*; namely, a group called out by God. Obviously, God calls every Christian into a local church to be a part of the body. The church is a diverse group of people whose life stories, burdens, and training facilitate different aspects of capturing, inviting, and directing others to Jesus. My life-on-life missional discipleship group of men consists of four business executives, one bricklayer, one SWAT team member, a computer geek or two, and various other particular callings. This motley redeemed "band of brothers" shares a similar burden, takes bullets for each other, and mobilizes one another for sacrificial service. We have fed the poor, comforted the children of prisoners, and witnessed to the lost. Such a community is a gift from God, and is found where Christians are running from an old way of sinful living, with an awakened sense of calling to Christ, and persevering toward the crown that Christ holds out for his saints.

---

[51] I was greatly influenced on this concept by Dan Allender's *The Healing Path: How The Hurts In Your Past Can Lead You To A More Abundant Life* (Colorado Springs, CO: WaterBrook Press, 1999), pp. 205, 211-236.

The threefold expression of Christians in the New Covenant connected together as a band of brothers and sisters, aware of their callings to Christ, is a powerful movement. It needs a place, however, to reach out on the streets of our communities. So, we ask, "Where's my place?" Calling's question is about a place God tells us to serve and belong. Why ask about place in the context of calling?

Place Matters

In ancient Greek society, the central gathering place was called the *agora*; it was the "place of commerce, information, and ideas." At the heart of the city, goods were sold, artisans interacted with others in their trade, and people gathered to debate political, philosophical, and theological matters. The *agora* was the Greek word for the streets.

Wherever people gather to conduct business, talk, eat, drink, and debate in the place God put you is your place. It may be a gym or a coffee shop, but these places exist in every community. Dan Allender exhorts Christians to go to such a place. He writes:

> Missiologists tell us that when a person comes to Christ, he loses most of his friendships with unbelievers within the first year. Seldom does conversion lead back into bars, coffee shops, and jazz clubs. But this was never God's intent. We're meant to be a new community, a holy priesthood that returns to the insipid, cold world as salt and light, flavor and warmth ... Instead we are meant to be in the midst of society, conducting business, writing plays, selling paintings, drinking coffee,

and infiltrating the world with faith, hope, and love.[52]

Although I have taught pastors in over twenty-five nations, there are plenty of opportunities to meet other people in the United States without the need for a translator. My wife, Karen, and I ate a feast over at our new friends' home. Abu and I met at the gym because I greeted him warmly. I pray while I run on the treadmill that God will give me people to win to Christ. When I met Abu from India for the first time, he was surprised because no one had befriended him since he had arrived in the United States two years ago.

I mentioned that I had been to India three times before and that I had been in his home city. Anyway, we exchanged phone numbers and the next day he said, "I went home, Bob, and told my wife that I finally have a friend! We want you to come to our home for a feast." We had a delightful time, eating with our fingers the delicious curry-seasoned gravy with chicken. This dear Muslim family in our community is on my heart, and we are friends whether they become Christians or not. This next week is our Christmas Eve service, and they are coming.

Here are a few simple ways to start pursuing community: Meet at least one person once a month for coffee. Set up a monthly phone call with a friend or colleague. Send a monthly email to a small group of trusted friends and colleagues just checking in and sharing what you're working on or struggling with. Start a life-on-life missional discipleship group to invest your life into other faithful men or women, who will then be able to invest in others. Ask a friend to pray for you at church or offer to pray for a friend in need.

---

[52] Dan Allender, *The Healing Path,* p. 241.

Why Keep Changing Places?

Today our culture is marked by impermanence. Thousands move every year and forfeit the opportunities for community in order to chase after the dream of social upward mobility. Permanence and continuity of place has been a great interest recently by various Christian thinkers.[53] Michael Horton wrote on the promiscuous soul in contemporary culture:

> Although we are used to identifying promiscuity with dissolute sexual behavior, it seems to capture the spirit of our age in more general terms … However all of this happened, there is no doubt that the loss of a solid sense of self has contributed to the promiscuity that marks our lives, including our callings.[54]

Wisdom teaches us that it is better to remain in one place and reap a richer harvest from seeds sown faithfully and annually for many, many years. "Trust in the Lord, and do good; dwell in the land," the Psalmist exhorts, "and cultivate faithful-ness" (Psalm 37:3). Trees take a long time to grow tall and beautiful. Children benefit from long-term friendships, and stories that matter to the soul have more than one short chapter after another and many plots. Paul told Pastor Timothy to remain in Ephesus to fulfill his charge (1 Timothy 1:3), and he instructed "each one to remain in the condition in which he was called" (1 Corinthians 7:20). One converted and famous author, T. S. Eliot, wrote, "On the whole, it would be better that the great

---

[53] See David Wells, *No Place for Truth* (Grand Rapids: Eerdmans, 1993), pp. 42–52, 76.

[54] Michael Horton, "How to Discern Your Calling," *Modern Reformation,* Vol. 8, Issue 3, p. 10.

majority of human beings should go on living in the place in which they were born."[55]

There is a tendency for Christians to move and leave the place God has put them as soon as a season of affliction arises. We are like Naomi's family in the beginning of the book of Ruth. Matthew Henry commented on this when he wrote:

> It is an evidence of a discontented, distrustful, unstable spirit, to be weary of the place in which God has set us, and to be for leaving it immediately whenever we meet with any uneasiness or inconvenience in it. It is folly to think of escaping that cross which, being laid in our way, we ought to pick up. It is our wisdom to make the best of that which is, for it is seldom that changing our place is mending it.[56]

Every place God calls us will have a cross laid out before us on the floor in the morning when we awake, but it is a way of life that sacrifices in love for the welfare of others in one place. In the end God gives us the joy of seeing how it all mattered in one place. One of my favorite names in the Bible comes from Joseph's life. When he was called to an unwanted place of affliction, he was called into marriage and fatherhood. He had two sons, and each was named for an aspect of his story in relation to his calling. One son was named *Ephraim*; "For God has made me fruitful in the land of affliction" (Genesis 41:52).

I love this because Joseph sensed his calling from childhood

---

[55] T. S. Eliot, *Notes Towards the Definition of Culture* (London: Faber and Faber, 1948), p. 52.
[56] Matthew Henry, "Book of Ruth" in *Matthew Henry Commentary On the Whole Bible* (Peabody, MA: Hendrickson Publishers, 1992), Volume Two, p. 198.

through dreams, but the path it took him on was one of suffering. Wherever God placed him to work, Joseph was afflicted. Hi prevocation at home was to check on his older brothers, who mistreated him and meant it for evil. This took him to work for Potiphar, where Potiphar's wife tried to lay with him, and then she falsely accused him. This led to his work in a prison where the keeper of the prison put Joseph in charge of all the prisoners, "but the Lord was with Joseph and showed him steadfast love" (Genesis 39:21). Finally, Joseph was exalted by the Pharaoh to become like a prime minister. Pharaoh said: "You shall be over my house, and all my people shall order themselves at your command. Only as regards the throne will I be greater than you" (Genesis 41:40). Joseph married, had sons, orchestrated reconciliation and healing for his family, and prospered in the land of his affliction. The hymn writer, John Newton composed the following hymn on suffering:

> I asked the Lord that I might grow
> In faith, and love, and every grace;
> Might more of His salvation know,
> And seek, more earnestly, His face.
>
> 'Twas He who taught me thus to pray,
> And He, I trust, has answered prayer!
> But it has been in such a way,
> As almost drove me to despair.
>
> I hoped that in some favored hour,
> At once He'd answer my request;
> And by His love's constraining pow'r,
> Subdue my sins, and give me rest.

Instead of this, He made me feel
The hidden evils of my heart;
And let the angry pow'rs of hell
Assault my soul in every part.

Yea more, with His own hand He seemed
Intent to aggravate my woe;
Crossed all the fair designs I schemed,
Blasted my gourds, and laid me low.

Lord, why is this, I trembling cried,
Wilt thou pursue thy worm to death?
"'Tis in this way, the Lord replied,
I answer prayer for grace and faith.

These inward trials I employ,
From self, and pride, to set thee free;
And break thy schemes of earthly joy,
That thou may'st find thy all in Me.[57]

Joseph didn't run from the places where God put him to fulfill his particular callings. He endured suffering and remained faithful to his calling. There was another man who suffered unjustly without running from affliction; namely, Jesus Christ. He finished his race set before Him, enduring the pain and despising the shame. God highly exalted Him, and put Him over all things.

What these old and contemporary writers are saying is that place matters to God, and we can trust that when we are called, He puts us in a place to have a lifelong impact. He expects us to remain in our place until we are released to another place, and called by

---

[57] John Newton, Olney Hymns (London: W. Oliver, 1779)

another people to serve in the context of community for a long period of time.

This chapter points us in the way of living out His calling on our lives in a threefold expression—as a prophet, priest, and a king; within a community of believers—a band of brothers and sisters; and in the place God put us. Place matters to God, as it should to us.

Discussion Group Questions:

1. What are you strongest at expressing—prophet, priest, or king? Where do you need to grow in your calling to Christ?
2. Do you think God is forming you into a band of brothers and sisters who share a kindred spirit with you in the sense of particular callings?
3. Where is your place? Where has God put you to live out your calling? How would you describe it? Where do people hang out in your community? How can you trust God to be more effective in your place?
4. Take time to prepare the template in the next chapter by writing out your sense of calling to Christ. Do not be afraid to share it with others because it will encourage others and help you clarify your sense of calling to Christ.

Chapter 6
Sharing Your Calling to Christ

This is really the most important part of the book, and the most transformational because it offers you the opportunity to share with others your sense of calling to Christ. It helps you to solidify it in your own words and identify the unique way God is calling you in the Christian life in a general way and in particular ways. You can see below there is a template designed for you to fill in the lines and to connect the dots. First, however, perhaps a few samples may assist you in writing out your sense of calling to Christ. The first is from an elder in a church, and the second is a woman married with grown children.

Sample Calling One

My Calling to Christ

My name is [Anonymous] and my calling to Christ flows out of my identity in Christ; a man created by him as a new creation, justified through Christ, adopted into the Father's family, and am sanctified/am being sanctified/and will be sanctified through the work of the Holy Spirit. I am a new creation in Christ, loved by Him, guided by

Him, protected by Him. I am one He never leaves nor forsakes, one He is for, one He has graciously called to join Him in His work.

I am His workmanship created in Christ to do good works predestined for me, works He has prepared for me to do, He being the author and finisher of my faith. With His enabling, resting in Him and His ability and guidance, I can do all things—both initiating works and working with others as we discern spiritually His leading.

God called me first and foremost to Christ, who clarifies my calling, to bring Him the glory that is due Him, to point others to Him, to have His power work through me in a way that only He can receive the glory, to walk intimately with Him so it is only His voice I recognize and honor and follow—to the exclusion of all others, to love Him with all my heart, soul, strength and mind.

My calling is unique and meaningful in my principal and peripheral works. He calls me to love others—my wife, my family, and His family and all peoples. He gives me avenues to do this through the relationships he provides, through the office of elder, and soon through the office of executive pastor, in community with others and with His enabling.

I am taking down, and removing by the power of the gospel, the following hindrances to hearing my calling to Christ—the lie that He counts me unworthy even though I stand in Christ, doubts that try to flow by the way that He answers my prayers—ways that leave me with question marks at times, the lie that He grows weary of forgiving me, and the temptation to place my trust in other gods, seeking comfort and rest there.

God is using the kairotic events in my life to direct me to fulfill His call on my life—both tragedy and redemptive ones. Tragedy is in the dysfunctional family I grew up in and the hurts it caused in all of us. How he redeems that through time to His glory, stopping cycles and ending sinful patterns. How He has saved me physically to the redemption of my family. How He has protected me and brought me through very difficult workplace circumstances.

What makes me weep for joy is seeing His redemptive work—His work of reconciliation in relationships and His power revealed to His glory—especially in revival. What makes me angry is seeing His children walk as captives in confusion and deception, short of the joy and blessing He has for them. What I love to do is worship Him in spirit and in truth—giving Him the glory in word and song and work.

The oracle in this season of my life, like mail to be delivered, is to me and to others—to rest in Him—coming alongside Him in His work—under His yoke—with joy and freedom.

God is calling me to capture His vision for spiritual discernment (as a king), which calls me to disrupt myself and my practices as well as those around me (as a prophet) and invite them (as a priest) to grace in order to call them out into a glorious future.

He has called me to this place, where I am finding contentment in knowing that He not only knows what is best for His kingdom and my calling, but also He knows how to contact me for a calling to another place or particular calling.

I am becoming more solid about who I am in Christ, more secure about my place in His world, and I want to live with intentionality for Christ until I receive from Him a legacy worth giving to the next generation.

Sample Calling Two

My Calling to Christ

My name is [Anonymous] and my calling to Christ flows out of my identity in Christ. I am a daughter of the King of Kings who has been forgiven and redeemed, and can now stand as righteous before my Lord (or climb into His lap) because of the righteousness of Christ imputed to me.

I am His workmanship, created in Christ to do good works predestined for me. So far, a majority of those works have focused on being a helpmate and friend to Fred, and a mom, teacher and disciple-maker to our kids. My role will change in the next few years as I retire from home-schooling, become an empty-nester and a mother-in-law, support my husband through a career change, and honor my aging parents. While I hope for thirty more years of living an abundant life in Christ, I confess that I feel more scared than excited about my future. So, I am eager to understand more of His calling on my life.

I am taking down and removing, by the power of the gospel, the major hindrances to hearing my calling to Christ... comparing myself to others, the idol of approval, and living under the "should" gun. I long to be free from these hindrances, and to be free to joyfully rest in Christ and live out the special calling God has just for me.

God is using the kairotic events in my life, both tragic and redemptive, to direct me to fulfill His call on my life. I have been relationally broken and devastated, but have experienced healing and new life breathed into the dry bones. What makes me angry and what makes me weep are the same... being emotionally hurt, seeing other people hurt, and seeing strained or broken relationships. What I love to do... I love this section because it frees me from the "should" gun!

My longings are: Casual ... I love to work at home with my hands. I love to keep our home organized, well run, and beautiful. I absolutely love, love, love to bake delicious desserts! I love to garden and do canning or freezing. I love to be outside, and to have people over for dinner. I love to make things beautiful and peaceful. Critical... I long to have deep, intimate relationships with my husband, our kids, and their future spouses. I long to be a godly grandma. I long to be available so I can give of myself to my family, parents, siblings and friends. Crucial ... or, where I long to have God come through. I long to know, at the depth of my soul, that: I am enough, I am loved and valuable, I am useful to God for His purposes, and I am free to be who He created me to be. I long to rest fully in His arms.

The oracle in this season of my life, like mail to be delivered, is to love and encourage. I am not naturally a king or prophet, but God has given me the heart to be a priest ... to comfort, to listen, and to invite hearts to cry out to God.

I am becoming more solid about who I am in Christ, more secure about my place in His world, and I want to live with intentionality for Christ until receive from Him a legacy worth giving to the next generation.

Your Turn: What is Your Calling to Christ?
(Please write out and share.)

My Calling to Christ

Write out your sense of calling in order to read in front of the group at our last meeting.

My name is _____ and my calling to Christ flows out of my identity in Christ ...

I am His workmanship created in Christ to do good works predestined for me ...

God called me first and foremost to Christ, who clarifies my calling ...

My calling is unique and meaningful in my principal and peripheral works …

I am taking down and removing by the power of the gospel the following hindrances to hearing my calling to Christ …

God is using the kairotic events in my life to direct me to fulfill His call on my life—both tragedy and redemptive ones …

What makes me weep is …

What makes me angry is …

What I love to do with humility is …

The oracle in this season of my life, like mail to be delivered, is …

God is calling me to capture His vision for _____ (as a king), which calls me to disrupt _____ (as a prophet) and invite _____ (as a priest) to grace in order to call them out into a glorious future.

He has called me to this place, where I am finding contentment in knowing that He not only knows what is best for His kingdom and my calling, but also He knows how to contact me for a calling to another place or particular calling.

I am becoming more solid about who I am in Christ, more secure about my place in His world, and I want to live with intentionality for Christ until I receive from Him a legacy worth giving to the next generation.

I recommend that you each share your sense of calling to Christ over a meal at someone's home, where after dinner each person shares with the group.

Conclusion
What's the Next Season of Spiritual Formation?

We have covered a lot of material with regard to discovering your calling to Christ. It is a process, and you have taken the first step. Over the years God will clarify this season of spiritual formation as you reread and reapply it to your life.

We have defined the Christian's calling to Christ, offered a theological foundation for calling, addressed eight hindrances to joy in your calling to Christ, sought to personalize your sense of calling to Christ, encouraged you to live it out in a threefold way in the context of community and place, and provided a template for you to write out and share your calling to Christ with others.

I would encourage you to participate in the whole series of Four Spiritual Seasons of Spiritual Formation—Identity in Christ, Calling to Christ, Intentionality for Christ, and Legacy from Christ. These four books are designed to shape you into a godly Christian is takes the fourfold seasons of the Christian life to heart.

The next two books are forthcoming under the same publisher, and you may benefit as well by going to my blog at http://www.identityinchrist.co

Please contact me for speaking engagements, or for help along the way.

Bibliography

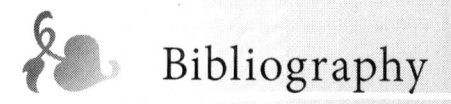

Dan Allender, *The Healing Path: How The Hurts In Your Past Can Lead You To A More Abundant Life* (Colorado Springs, CO: WaterBrook Press, 1999).

Robert Bly, *Iron John: A Book about Men* (New York: Vintage Books, 1990).

Dietrich Bonhoeffer, *Letters and Papers from Prison* (New York, NY: The Macmillan Company, 1953, repr. 1967).

Frederick Buechner, *Wishful Thinking: A Seeker's ABC* (New York, NY: HarperCollins, 1973).

John Calvin, *Institutes of the Christian Religion* (Philadelphia, PA: The Westminster Press, 1960), Two Volumes.

Larry Crabb, *InsideOut* (Colorado Springs, CO: NavPress, 1988).

Fyodor Dostoevsky, *The Brothers Karamazov* (The Inquisitor) is quoted in Os Guiness, *The Call: Finding and Fulfilling the Central Purpose of Your Life* (Nashville, TN: Word Publishing, 1998).

T. S. Eliot, *Notes Towards the Definition of Culture* (London: Faber and Faber, 1948).

Zack Eswine, *Sensing Jesus: Life and Ministry as a Human Being* (Wheaton, IL: Crossway, 2013).

Edwin H. Friedman, *A Failure of Nerve: Leadership in the Age of the Quick Fix* (Seabury Books, 2007).

Os Guiness, *The Call: Finding and Fulfilling the Central Purpose of Your Life* (Nashville, TN: Word Publishing, 1998).

Matthew Henry, "Book of Ruth" in *Matthew Henry Commentary On the Whole Bible* (Peabody, MA: Hendrickson Publishers, 1992), Two Volumes.

Michael Horton, "How to Discern Your Calling" in *Modern Reformation*, Vol. 8, Issue 3, pp. 8–13.

Timothy Keller, "Vocation: Discerning Your Calling," www.redeemercitytocity.com

_____, *Every Good Endeavor: Connecting Your Work to God's Work* (New York, NY: Dutton, 2012).

Abraham Kuyper: A Centennial Reader, ed. James D. Bratt (Grand Rapids, MI: Eerdmans, 1998).

C. S. Lewis, "The Inner Ring" in *The Weight of Glory and Other Addresses* (New York, NY: Simon and Schuster, 1975, repr. 1980).

_____, *Mere Christianity* (San Francisco, CA: Harper, 2001).

_____, *The Silver Chair* (New York: NY: Harper Trophy, 1981).

Martin Luther, *Three Treatises* (Fortress: 1970).

_____, *Luther's Works*, Volume 44.

_____, *The Babylonian Captivity of the Church* (1520).

_____, Jaroslav Pelikan, editor, *Luther's Works* (St. Louis, MO: Concordia Publishing House, 1955).

Catherine Marshall, *A Man Called Peter: The Story of Peter Marshall* (Grand Rapids, MI: Baker, 1951).

David Martyn Lloyd-Jones, *Healing and the Scriptures* (Thomas Nelson, 1982).

Henri J. M. Nouwen, *Life of the Beloved: Spiritual Living in a Secular World* (New York, NY: Crossroad Publishing Company, 2002).

_____, *The Wounded Healer: Ministry in Contemporary Society* (New York, NY: Doubleday, 1972).

_____, *Here and Now: Living in the Spirit* (Danvers, MA: The Crossroad Publishing Company, 1994), Kindle Locations 1275–1278. Kindle Edition.

William Perkins, *A Treatises of the Vocations or Callings of Men* is quoted in Os Guiness, *The Call: Finding and Fulfilling the Central Purpose of Your Life* (Nashville, TN: Word Publishing, 1998).

Eugene Peterson, *A Long Obedience in the Same Direction* (Downers Grove, IL: InterVarsity Press, 1980).

Josef Piper, *Leisure: The Basis of Culture* (San Francisco, CA: Ignatius Press, 2009).

Dorothy Sayers, *Creed or Chaos* (New York, NY: Harcourt, Brace, 1949).

Francis A. Schaeffer, *The Complete Works of Francis A. Schaeffer: A Christian Worldview* (Wheaton, IL: Crossway Books, 1982), Five Volumes.

Robert Davis Smart, *Embracing Your Identity in Christ: Renouncing Lies and Foolish Strategies* (Bloomington, IN: Westbow Press, 2017).

_____, *Intentionality for Christ: What's My Aim?* (Bloomington, IN: Westbow Press, 2017).

_____, *Legacy from Christ: What's My Message?* (Bloomington, IN: Westbow Press, 2017).

_____, Review of Michael Horton's *Ordinary: Sustainable Faith in a Radical, Restless World* (Grand Rapids, MI: Zondervan, 2014. 224 pp. http://themelios.thegospelcoalition.org/review/ordinary-sustainable-faith-in-a-radical-restless-world-michael-horton

Christian Smith with Patricia Snell, *Souls in Transition: The Religious & Spiritual Lives of Emerging Adults* (New York: Oxford University Press, 2008).

William Stafford, *The Way It Is: New and Selected Poems* (Minneapolis, MN: Graywolf Press, 1998).

David Wells, *No Place for Truth* (Grand Rapids: Eerdmans, 1993).

Ben Wirtherington, *Work: The Meaning of Your Life* (Grand Rapids, MI: Eerdmans, 2011).

Appendix
Practicing the Spiritual Discipline of Solitude

Practicing solitude is crucial to spiritual formation, especially for a calling group.

1. Why practice the spiritual discipline of solitude?

Blaise Pascal, whose calling to Christ was seen as a remarkable scientist and Christian theologian, wrote in his Pensees (section 136): "All unhappiness of men arises from one single fact, that they cannot stay quietly in their room." Pascal argues that our default mode is to turn to "diversions" to distract us from our misery:

> Hence it comes people so much love noise and stir; hence it comes that the prison is so horrible a punishment; hence it comes that the pleasure of solitude is a thing incomprehensible.

We have, however, "another instinct, a remnant of the greatness of our original nature, which teaches that happiness in reality consists only in rest, and not being stirred up." We believe that the way to happiness in one's calling is through daily solitude in Word and prayer. Henri Nouwen wrote: "Without solitude it is virtually impossible to live a spiritual life ... we do not take the spiritual life seriously if we do not set aside some time to be with God and listen to Him."[58]

2. What does the author mean by solitude as a spiritual discipline?

To enter into solitude by Word and prayer is to intentionally seek to commune with God. It is to come into God's presence to listen and respond to His call and invitation for intimacy with you. It is to practice taking His call on your life seriously enough to hush the noise in your life, to cease striving, to pull away from your preoccupations with people and work for a scheduled time in order to hear His voice.

> Read Psalm 131
>
> *O Lord, my heart is not lifted up;*
> *my eyes are not raised too high;*
>
> *I do not occupy myself with things*
> *too great and too marvelous for me.*
>
> *But I have calmed and quieted my soul,*
> *like a weaned child with its mother;*
> *like a weaned child is my soul within me.*
>
> *O Israel, hope in the Lord*
> *from this time forth and forevermore.*

Matthew Henry, commenting on John 1:19–37, wrote: "A place of silence and solitude, out of the noise of the world and the hurry of its

---

[58] Quoted in Ruth Hailey Barton

business; the more retired we are from the tumult of secular affairs the better prepared we are to hear from God."

3. How can we practice the spiritual discipline of solitude?

Five Basic Steps to Intimacy with God and Joy in Calling:

1. Quiet every possible voice and anxious thought, and have no other gods before Him. Breathe and listen.

2. Remind yourself of your identity in Christ; i.e. who He says you are. Pull out your Identity in Christ sheet or simply preach the gospel to yourself as best as you can. Name anxious thoughts and take them captive (2 Corinthians 10:4–5).

3. Wait for your soul to emerge from hiding (in the context of a noisy and broken world) with a question to bring to God. Ask Him about your sense of call to Him; about the abundant life He came to give you; about your place in the kingdom; about why He gifted you in a particular manner; about how He will use tragedies and redemptive moments in your life; and about your deepest longings.

4. Read, meditate (ponder), and talk to God over the Bible. Take delight in His works of creation, providence, and redemption. Enjoy His Word! Delight yourself in the Lord, and He will give you the desires of your heart (Psalm 37:4).

5. Pray and write out creative ideas and plans inspired by being in His Presence (James 1:5; Proverbs 8).

Made in the USA
Coppell, TX
14 February 2020